THE SKILLFUL HUNTSMAN

visual development of a Grimm tale at Art Center College of Design

KHANG LE   MIKE YAMADA   FELIX YOON   SCOTT ROBERTSON

designstudio|PRESS

dedication

This book is dedicated to aspiring concept artists everywhere.

Art Direction: Scott Robertson
Graphic Design: fancygraphics
Web Site: www.fancygraphics.net

Layout Production: Marsha Stevenson
Text Editor: Anna Skinner

"The Skillful Huntsman" from
The Complete Grimm's Fairy Tales,
trans. Margaret Hunt [1884], New York, 1944;
rev. James Stern, New York, 1972.

Published by Design Studio Press
8577 Higuera Street
Culver City, CA 90232

Web Site: www.designstudiopress.com
E-mail: Info@designstudiopress.com

10 9 8 7 6 5 4

Printed in China
Fourth Printing, May 2011

Paperback ISBN 0-972-6676-4-4
Hardback ISBN 0-972-6676-8-7

Library of Congress Control Number:
2005921544

contents

foreword

THE BROTHERHOOD OF GRIMM

What you hold in your hands is very old, and very new.

When "The Skillful Huntsman" was first written down in a book of fairy tales by the Brothers Grimm, there was no internet, no movies, no television, and no radio. They had no keyboards to type it on, or indoor light bulbs to type it by. About the latest fun thing was tinned food, except no one thought to invent the can opener, so maybe it wasn't that fun after all. It was an era of wars and horror stories, such as those of Edgar Allen Poe, and Mary Shelley's *Frankenstein*.

Even back then, "The Skillful Huntsman" was a grandaddy of a tale. Storytellers first whispered it over looms and fires in the time of the Black Death. A medieval shocker full of decapitation, drawing and quartering, and the chopping of tongues, it was a verbal echo of the violence and danger in our pre-traffic light world.

The artists who have revisited the Brothers Grimm tale in the pages of this book are all very new. Most of them were born long after *Star Wars*, or *Star Trek*, or the ubiquitous email. Many of their images were painted on a computer, indoor light bulbs extinguished because of the glare. Yet theirs is also, in its own way, a dark time, a time of devastating wars and global terror, decapitations and the silencing of tongues. Perhaps their choice of story is also an echo of the darkness and danger in the world around them.

Fairy tales have always been a safe place to examine dark things. Over the centuries, we have pulled their teeth, removed the sharp and nasty bits just in case—God forbid—a child might read them.

To the artists who have created this wonderful book, these young Brothers Grimm, who have re-imagined this dark little tale in all its original fury, I salute you. You make us proud.

Iain McCaig
Concept Artist (*Star Wars, Peter Pan, Harry Potter and The Goblet of Fire*).

introduction

Several years ago I decided to find a way to document the creative visualization process we traverse within the entertainment design projects here at Art Center College of Design. I have been fortunate enough to teach at Art Center for almost ten years now. While teaching an advanced entertainment studio, I had the pleasure of working with three very talented students: Khang Le, Mike Yamada, and Felix Yoon. One of my new ventures is publishing unique design and art books under the Design Studio Press imprint. My desire to share the amazing things that were occurring in my studio classes at Art Center led me to the creation of this book.

I pitched the idea of a student visual development book to Khang, Mike, Felix, and Art Center. Everyone agreed it would be an interesting experiment. The project began with the students and myself setting out to find a short story from years past that we could visually develop over the course of one fourteen week Art Center term. I wanted the book to focus on the earliest stage of visual development—what typically occurs behind closed doors in the art departments of feature films or video games. We have all seen the end results of these efforts in *The Art of...* books put out with the release of a new film. Because of my continued disappointment with the quality of these various books, and the lack of early design directions being presented therein, we made it our focus to show all of our early design sketches and to end each chapter with multiple design solutions for the subject of that chapter. Since we all worked in our own studios and only met once a week, I wanted the students to freely explore placing the characters of the story into any time period they wished, and to assume any level of technological sophistication or lack thereof for the society they were imagining for the story.

We chose "The Skillful Huntsman" by the Brothers Grimm. We would design the environments, characters, props, and vehicles.

After reviewing the story we came up with a list of specific design topics to pursue over the term. The list became the chapters of this book. Each chapter shares with you the creative process we applied to all the topics we pulled from the story. In keeping with the desire to share the earliest sketches in the creative process, you will see a wide variety of designs throughout each chapter. We employed a very common visual development practice of drawing many small thumbnail sketches to quickly flesh out ideas, and then shared these with each other to inspire us to keep pushing in new directions. The overall critiques I gave during the development of the designs were mainly to drive the students to push their originality in more directions. Usually, when anyone starts to design an object from their imagination, they draw what they already know and what they have already seen. We all live on the same planet, and with the widespread availability of the Internet and movies we are all looking at the same things most of the time. A designer can be sent down the path of creating something more original by emptying his or her visual library through producing a high volume of fast thumbnail sketches. During this process a designer will probably draw the same things over and over and feel very bored. But working through the boredom can frequently allow for moments of inspiration and the exploration of truly original ideas and styles.

I must add, as an educator, I am very pleased with the quality of the design ideas and the high level of the art displayed by these three very talented students. I often joke with them that they are starting their careers in reverse, by my publishing their student work in this book. They have accomplished a very strong block of work that I hope will inspire other students and professionals to create and publish works of their own, to share with the rest of us.

Thanks to Khang, Mike, Felix, and Art Center College of Design for all of their hard work and support along the way.

Scott Robertson.

Winter 2004 in Los Angeles.

Scott Robertson

Art Center Instructor
Design Studio Press Founder

KHANG LE

FELIX YOON

MIKE YAMADA

Khang Le was born in Saigon, Vietnam in 1981. When he was ten, his family moved to Los Angeles, California, and Le immersed himself in the world of comic books. During high school, a friend introduced him to the Art Center College of Design in Pasadena. At the same time, *The Art of Star Wars, Episode I: The Phantom Menace* came out, and making a living as a concept artist for the entertainment industry become Le's aspiration. In 2000, he got accepted to Art Center, where he had the opportunity to refine his skills to freelance for various entertainment mediums, including games, movies, music videos, and publishing. He has recently graduated and is currently traveling the world and considering all of his professional options.

Felix Yoon was born in Pennsylvania in 1982, where he spent his childhood, and later relocated to South Korea. He moved to California as he entered high school. It wasn't until senior year when Yoon decided to take art seriously as a possible occupation. After high school he entered Art Center College of Design, where he graduated with honors with a BFA in illustration. He started working as a concept artist for video games and now works as a visual development artist at DreamWorks Animation.

Michael Yamada was born and raised in Pasadena, California. Originally intending to be a graphic designer, Yamada attended a local community college and changed his course of study after discovering a book of *Star Wars* production art. He transferred to Art Center College of Design where in 2003 he graduated with honors with a BS degree in product design with a emphasis on entertainment design. He has spent the year after his graduation employed as a visual development artist at DreamWorks Animation, and working on a variety of freelance projects. He also teaches at Otis College of Art and Design.

Khang Le
khangle81@yahoo.com

Felix Yoon
felixyoon@hotmail.com

Mike Yamada
myamada@gmail.com

01

02

03

SCOTT ROBERTSON

Scott Robertson studied transportation design and product design at Art Center College of Design, and graduated with honors in April 1990. He immediately opened a consulting firm in San Francisco, where he designed a variety of consumer products, the majority being durable medical goods and sporting goods. He has been teaching at Art Center College of Design since 1995, first with a year and a half stint at Art Center Europe in Vevey, Switzerland (now closed), and then in Pasadena, California.

In the years since returning from Europe, Robertson's clients have included BMW subsidiary Design-works/USA, Bell Sports, Raleigh Bicycles, Mattel Toys, Patagonia, Scifi Lab, 3DO, *Minority Report* feature film, Nike, Troxel, Rock Shox, Universal Studios, OVO, Black Diamond, Angel Studios, Rockstar Games, and Fiat to name a few.

Dedicated to art and design education, Robertson founded the publishing company Design Studio Press. The company's first book, *Concept Design*, is a collection of original artwork by seven of the top concept artists working in Hollywood, with a foreword by Francis Ford Coppola. *Concept Design 2* is due out in mid-2005. Other books published by his company are *Monstruo: The Art of Carlos Huante, and Quantum Dreams: The Art of Stephan Martinière.* The biggest seller to date is *AVP-Alien vs. Predator: The Creature Effects of A.D.I.*

Robertson recently art directed 240 illustrations for Mattel's Hot Wheels AcceleRacers collectible card game. He also authored a new book, *How to Draw Cars the Hot Wheels Way.* Recently, Design Studio Press has teamed with The Gnomon Workshop to create a library of "how to" DVDs. Robertson himself has instructed on seven DVDs, focusing on drawing and rendering techniques for industrial and entertainment designers. He has co-produced an additional 36 DVDs with various top artists, designers, and instructors, including Syd Mead. To view all the titles currently available, visit www.thegnomonworkshop.com.

Scott Robertson
scott@designstudiopress.com

04

THE SKILLFUL HUNTSMAN by the Brothers Grimm

There was once a young fellow who had learned the trade of locksmith, and told his father he would now go out into the world to seek his fortune. "Very well," said the father, "I am quite content with that," and gave him some money for his journey. So he traveled about and looked for work. After a time he resolved not to follow the trade of locksmith anymore, for he no longer liked it, but he took a fancy for hunting.

Then there met him in his rambles a huntsman dressed in green, who asked whence he came and whither he was going. The youth said he was a locksmith's apprentice, but that the trade no longer pleased him, and he had a liking for huntsmanship, would he teach it to him?

"Oh, yes," said the huntsman, "if you will go with me." Then the young fellow went with him, apprenticed himself to him for some years, and learnt the art of hunting. After this he wished to try his luck elsewhere, and the huntsman gave him nothing in the way of payment but an airgun, which had, however, this property, that it hit its mark without fail whenever he shot with it. Then he set out and found himself in a very large forest, which he could not get to the end of in one day. When evening came he seated himself in a high tree in order to escape from the wild beasts.

Towards midnight, it seemed to him as if a tiny little light glimmered in the distance. Then he looked down through the branches towards it, and kept well in his mind where it was. But in the first place he took off his hat and threw it down in the direction of the light, so that he might go to the hat as a mark when he had descended. He got down and went to his hat, put it on again and went straight forwards. The farther he went, the larger the light grew, and when he got close to it he saw that it was an enormous fire, and that three giants were sitting by it, who had an ox on the spit, and were roasting it. Presently one of them said: "I must just taste if the meat will soon be fit to eat," and pulled a piece off, and was about to put it in his mouth when the huntsman shot it out of his hand.

"Well, really," said the giant, "if the wind has not blown the bit out of my hand!" and helped himself to another. But when he was just about to bite into it, the huntsman again shot it away from him. On this the giant gave the one who was sitting next him a box on the ear, and cried angrily: "Why are you snatching my piece away from me?"

"I have not snatched it away," said the other, "A sharpshooter must have shot it away from you."

The giant took another piece, but again could not keep it in his hand, for the huntsman shot it out. Then the giant said: "That must be a good shot to shoot the bit out of one's very mouth, such an one would be useful to us."

And he cried aloud: "Come here, you sharpshooter, seat yourself at the fire beside us and eat your fill, we will not hurt you; but if you will not come, and we have to bring you by force, you are a lost man!"

On this the youth went up to them and told them he was a skilled huntsman, and that whatever he aimed at with his gun, he was certain to hit. Then they said if he would go with them he should be well treated, and they told him that outside the forest there was a great lake, behind which stood a tower, and in the tower was imprisoned a lovely princess, whom they wished very much to carry off.

"Yes," said he, "I will soon get her for you."
Then they added: "But there is still something else, there is a tiny little dog, which begins to bark directly any one goes near, and as soon as it barks every one in the royal palace wakens up, for this reason we cannot get there; can you undertake to shoot it dead?"

"Yes," said he, "that will be quite fun for me."
After this he got into a boat and rowed over the lake, and as soon as he landed, the little dog came running out, and was about to bark, but the huntsman took his airgun and shot it dead.

When the giants saw that, they rejoiced, and thought they already had the king's daughter safe, but the huntsman wished first to see how matters stood, and told them that they must stay outside until he called them. Then he went into the castle, and all was perfectly quiet within, and every one was asleep. When he opened the door of the first room, a sword was hanging on the wall which was made of pure silver, and there was a golden star on it, and the name of the king, and on a table near it lay a sealed letter which he broke open, and inside it was written that whosoever had the sword could kill everything which opposed him. So he took the sword from the wall, hung it at his side and went onwards: then he entered the room where the king's daughter was lying sleeping, and she was so beautiful that he stood still and, holding his breath, looked at her.

He thought to himself: "How can I give an innocent maiden into the power of the wild giants, who have evil in their minds?" He looked about further, and under the bed stood a pair of slippers, on the right slipper was her father's name with a star, and on the left her own name with a star. She wore also a large scarf of silk embroidered with gold, and on the right side was her father's name, and on the left her own, all in golden letters.

Then the huntsman took a pair of scissors and cut the right corner off, and put it in his knapsack, and then he also took the right slipper with the king's name, and thrust that in. Now the maiden still lay sleeping, and she was quite sewn into her night-dress, and he cut a morsel from this also, and thrust it in with the rest, but he did all without touching her.

Then he went forth and left her lying asleep undisturbed, and he came to the gate again, the giants were still standing outside waiting for him, and expecting that he was bringing the princess. But he cried to them that they were to come in, for the maiden was already in their power, that he could not open the gate to them, but there was a hole through which they must creep. Then the first approached, and the huntsman wound the giant's hair round his hand, pulled the head in, and cut it off at one stroke with his sword, and then drew the rest of him in. He called to the second and cut his head off likewise, and then he killed the third also, and he was well pleased that he had freed the beautiful maiden from her enemies, and he cut out their tongues and put them in his knapsack.

Then thought he: "I will go home to my father and let him see what I have already done, and afterwards I will travel about the world; the luck which God is pleased to grant me will easily find me."

But when the king in the castle awoke, he saw the three giants lying there dead. So he went into the sleeping-room of his daughter, awoke her, and asked who could have killed the giants? Then said she: "Dear father, I know not, I have been asleep." But when she arose and would have put on her slippers, the right one was gone. When she looked at her scarf it was cut, and the right corner was missing, and when she looked at her nightgown a piece was cut out of it. The king summoned his whole court together, soldiers and every one else who was there, and asked who had set his daughter at liberty, and killed the giants.

Now it happened that he had a captain, who was one-eyed and a hideous man, and he said that he had done it. Then the old king said that as he had accomplished this, he should marry his daughter. But the maiden said: "Rather than marry him, dear father, I will go away into the world as far as my legs can carry me."

But the king said that if she would not marry him she should take off her royal garments and wear peasant's clothing, and go forth, and that she should go to a potter, and begin a trade in earthen vessels. So she put off her royal apparel, and went to a potter and borrowed crockery enough for a stall, and she promised him also that if she had sold it by the evening, she would pay for it. Then the king said she was to seat herself in a corner with it and sell it, and he arranged with some peasants to drive over it with their carts, so that everything should be broken into a thousand pieces. When therefore the king's daughter had placed her stall in the street, by came the carts, and broke all she had into tiny fragments. She began to weep and said: "Alas, how shall I ever pay for the pots now?"

The king, however, had wished by this to force her to marry the captain; but instead of that, she again went to the potter, and asked him if he would lend to her once more. He said, "No," she must first pay for what she already had.

Then she went to her father and cried and lamented, and said she would go forth into the world. Then said he: "I will have a little hut built for you in the forest outside, and in it you shall stay all your life long and cook for every one, but you shall take no money for it."

When the hut was ready, a sign was hung on the door whereon was written: "To-day given, to-morrow sold." There she remained a long time, and it was rumored about the world that a maiden was there who cooked without asking for payment, and that this was set forth on a sign outside her door.

The huntsman heard it likewise, and thought to himself: "That would suit you. You are poor, and have no money." So he took his airgun and his knapsack, wherein all the things which he had formerly carried away with him from the castle as tokens of his truthfulness were still lying, and went into the forest, and found the hut with the sign: "To-day given, to-morrow sold." He had put on the sword with which he had cut off the heads of the three giants, and thus entered the hut, and ordered something to eat to be given to him. He was charmed with the beautiful maiden, who was indeed as lovely as any picture.

She asked him whence he came and whither he was going, and he said: "I am roaming about the world." Then she asked him where he had got the sword, for that truly her father's name was on it. He asked her if she were the king's daughter. "Yes," answered she. "With this sword," said he, "did I cut off the heads of three giants." And he took their tongues out of his knapsack in proof. Then he also showed her the slipper, and the corner of the scarf, and the piece of the night-dress.

Hereupon she was overjoyed, and said that he was the one who had delivered her. On this they went together to the old king, and fetched him to the hut, and she led him into her room, and told him that the huntsman was the man who had really set her free from the giants. And when the aged king saw all the proofs of this, he could no longer doubt, and said that he was very glad he knew how everything had happened, and that the huntsman should have her to wife, on which the maiden was glad at heart. Then she dressed the huntsman as if he were a foreign lord, and the king ordered a feast to be prepared. When they went to table, the captain sat on the left side of the king's daughter, but the huntsman was on the right, and the captain thought he was a foreign lord who had come on a visit. When they had eaten and drunk, the old king said to the captain that he would set before him something which he must guess.

"Supposing someone said that he had killed the three giants and he were asked where the giants' tongues were, and he were forced to go and look, and there were none in their heads. How could that have happened?" The captain said: "Then they cannot have had any."
"Not so," said the king.
"Every animal has a tongue," and then he likewise asked what punishment should be meted out to anyone who made such an answer. The captain replied: "He ought to be torn in pieces."

Then the king said he had pronounced his own sentence, and the captain was put in prison and then torn in four pieces; but the king's daughter was married to the huntsman. After this he brought his father and mother, and they lived with their son in happiness, and after the death of the old king he received the kingdom.

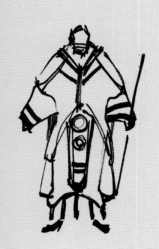 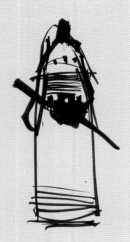   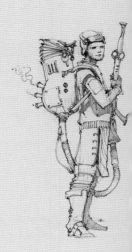

01 HUNTSMAN

HUNTSMAN

Felix: I began by making many small thumbnail sketches. At this stage I explored lots of ideas and directions and tried not to limit myself. All I knew specifically was that I wanted the hunter to have somewhat of an Asian styling in his costume.

Scott: Knowing where Felix wanted to take this early exploration, the thumbnail sketches here show a very broad range of shape and graphic design. When you look closely at several of the sketches, you can see a nice use of the lost line technique and a strong use of positive and negative shapes to make the costume of the character interesting to the viewer.

Lost line technique is the use of negative space to indicate the continuation of a line or edge, without drawing the line itself. A good example is the pant leg of sketch number four on line three.

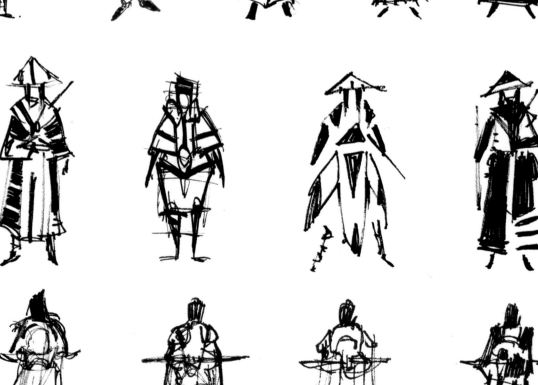

FELIX YOON

FELIX YOON

HUNTSMAN

Mike: I often start a character design with quite a few quick exploratory sketches. I use it as a way to get all the cliché and preconceived ideas out of my system. When doing these sketches, I thought mostly about patterns and shapes, and tried to give a sense of history and culture. Things like realism and proportion were secondary and were mostly ignored as design was a top priority.

These were done with a Japanese brush pen, which I learned to use during the process of making this book. This pen made it difficult to add small details and helped me to stay focused on general design.

Scott: With the focus of our project being design and not illustration, Mike's creation of many designs through thumbnail sketches is a great way to empty your existing visual library. Like Felix, Mike is not afraid to experiment with strong positive and negative shapes using this rapid sketching technique.

MIKE YAMADA

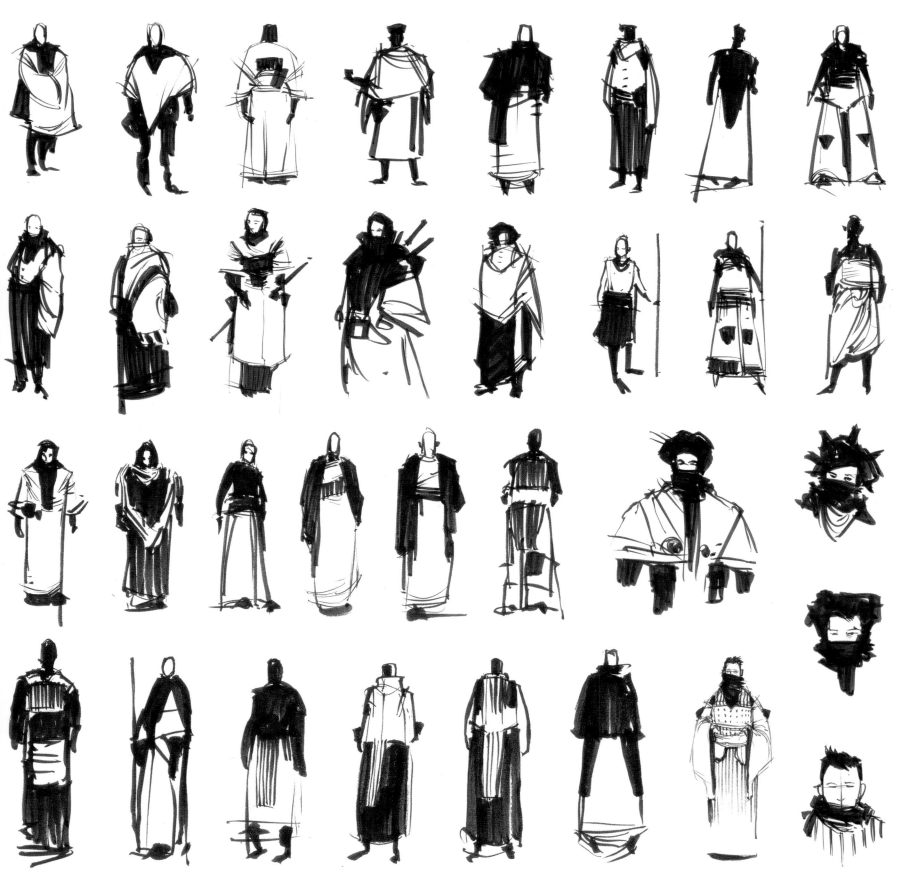

MIKE YAMADA

HUNTSMAN

Mike: Here, I went with a silhouette approach for the design of the huntsman. It allowed me to think of the outermost shape. When interior detail is omitted, you need to focus more on making the outer shape interesting and unique. It frees your mind and pen to create things that you would not do when building from the inside out.

Scott: I'm a big fan of this type of technique when developing any shape of your own design. You can see how powerful it is to the first quick "read" of a form. When you stand at some distance from an object, whether it be a car, person, or building, your first impression of that object is its silhouette. This technique is a lot of fun, and since you do not need to worry about perspective drawing or line quality you can really work fast and let your imagination run to create a large range of shapes and designs.

MIKE YAMADA

MIKE YAMADA

HUNTSMAN

Mike: I began these sketches wanting to establish a bulky feeling for the character of the huntsman. I used a traditional line drawing technique here. By changing my sketching style from the previous pages, it freed me to explore a wide variety of possibilities for the design. Partway through, I focused on a specific component of the design, the helmet/headpiece, and worked from there to complete the entire piece. These sketches go in a variety of directions, ranging from whimsical to more serious sci-fi/fantasy.

Scott: Throughout the term I stressed over and over the importance of originality in what the students were designing. I think Mike's variations on the headpieces show a good range of design aesthetics, and they demonstrate to us, the audience, how many ways the same character can be interpreted.

MIKE YAMADA

MIKE YAMADA

HUNTSMAN

Khang: I usually begin my character designs by doodling pages of thumbnails to find ideas. I'm looking for interesting shapes and silhouettes that will help to describe the character. One way to find interesting designs is by looking at abstract shapes around you. I often find new ideas in strange places, like a water stain on the floor or by turning recognizable objects upside down. Drawing at a very small scale prevents me from rendering tiny details that are unnecessary at this early stage. Also, it is economical for clients and directors to see a range of designs before committing time to any specific one.

Scott: Again, here you can see a wide range of original design ideas for the skillful huntsman. Using a slightly different technique than Mike and Felix, Khang works in more details early by sketching with more lines and at a slightly larger scale.

KHANG LE

KHANG LE

HUNTSMAN

Mike: I took some of my favorite silhouette sketches, and placed tracing paper over the top. Then I sketched options for the interior details with a pen or a pencil. You can see that any one silhouette has many options for the costume's details. Again, by working from the outside in, you can come upon unique designs that you might not have thought of if you'd sketched from the inside out.

Scott: I'm really glad Mike took his straight silhouette drawings to this next step. Many times students will do hundreds of small silhouette sketches but not know how to really use them to improve and move along their design development. This spread of pages nicely illustrates the infinite possibilities that lie within each silhouette drawing.

MIKE YAMADA

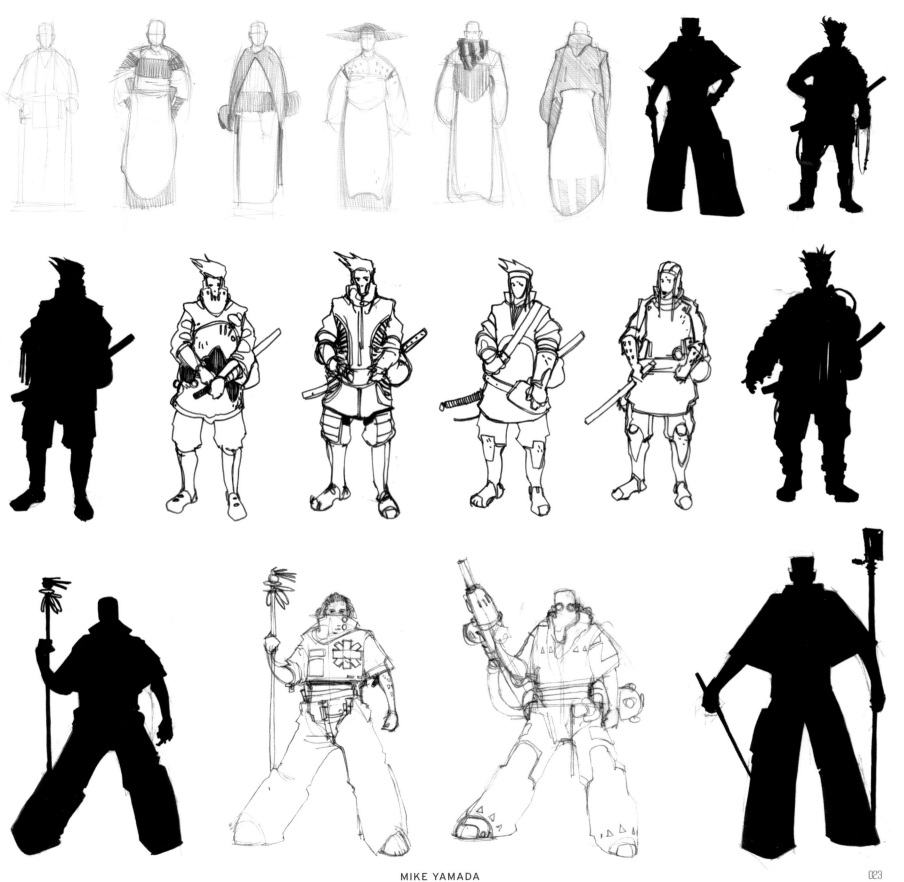

MIKE YAMADA

HUNTSMAN

Felix: These sketches are a bit more developed from the early thumbnail stage. I'm still pushing the idea of giving him long drapery. The sketches have gotten larger than in the thumbnail stage but I'm still keeping them loose. I used a chisel-tip pen to achieve a brush look.

Scott: These sketches demonstrate that by successfully mixing various genres a designer can come up with a fresh and new aesthetic that nevertheless feels familiar and accessible. You can see that Felix is still relying heavily on a strong use of graphic design applied to his huntsman's costume. By using a large chisel-tip calligraphy pen, he created a nice sense of movement, activity, and texture our mind's eye will fill in as a material change.

FELIX YOON

FELIX YOON

HUNTSMAN

Khang: Once the basic silhouette is established, the next stage is the rough sketching. These drawings are larger, so the smaller details can be given more attention. Everything the character carries can help tell a story about him. Story suggests design, and design can also spark new ideas for story. The metallic goggles with thin slits on the sketch above suggest a world with a fiery sun. On the sketch to the right of this, he has a patch on his shoulder. In the story, it might be a piece of fabric from his late grandfather.

Scott: The connection of story and design is one of the most important things an entertainment designer should work on. All design decisions should be made to support the story and reinforce the believability of the characters. As Khang mentioned above, sometimes new dimensions to the story can be discovered through the design phase of the project. Doing a variety and large volume of drawings is a key way to explore many possibilities during this phase.

KHANG LE

HUNTSMAN

Mike: On the left page I took one of my silhouette drawings, scanned it into Photoshop, worked back into the shape with just a white brush at first, and then progressively added some other values. This shape/value approach to design leads me to different results than what is shown on the right page, which is a line-based approach from the same starting point.

Scott: I think this is a really strong spread by Mike. Quite often I observe students doing hundreds of thumbnail silhouettes and then they do nothing with them. They move on to doing more finished drawings and lose the dynamics of the original sketch. On this page you can see that by using Photoshop, Mike is able to work directly into his original thumbnail sketch. By observing each sketch closely you can see how the same silhouette can be interpreted in many different ways. On the opposite page, I really like the graphic design and detail design exploration Mike has done. It is also fun to explore whether a silhouette sketch is a front or rear view, as seen in the first two sketches on that page.

MIKE YAMADA

MIKE YAMADA

HUNTSMAN

Mike: Here I continued with variations over one silhouette in further design exploration. I focused on shape, pattern, and simple motifs. On the accompanying page are two color roughs exploring the designs in slightly more detail.

Scott: As mentioned in the introduction, this project was intended to demonstrate the large range of possibilities one story could hold. What you see on the opposite page are two directions that Mike has proposed for the skillful huntsman. I think both work well, and it is easy to see how he arrived at these design directions from the work on the previous pages.

MIKE YAMADA

MIKE YAMADA

HUNTSMAN

Khang: Fantastical design is a juggling act between familiarity and strangeness. Make an alien character too alien and the audience won't relate to it. This is one of the reasons why most alien designs in movies have human features. For the huntsman, all the details are recognizable, but they're placed out of context. By bringing together elements that don't belong together and making them work with each other, new designs are made.

Scott: Khang is right on the money here; if you go too far out with your design direction, then no one can formulate an opinion about it. The normal guidelines for critique and judgment of whether or not the design resonates with the viewer cannot be used. It is easy to do different-looking designs for the sake of being different, but very hard to do different- and better-looking designs than we have ever seen before. This of course becomes the goal of any good concept designer: the balance between the foreign and the familiar.

KHANG LE

KHANG LE

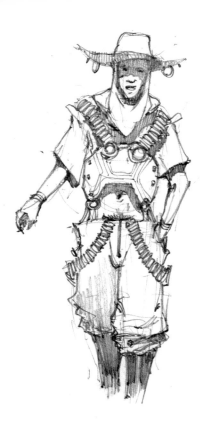

HUNTSMAN

Khang: I like using a pencil for most of my designs. It is a forgiving medium, but flexible enough to communicate most visual forms. I also sketch very loosely, with the intention of creating random marks. These "mistakes" can turn into unique details that I would not have thought about otherwise. People call them "happy accidents," but I prefer to think of them as controlled chaos. It's like staring at the clouds and seeing bunnies, or giant robots with lasers!

Scott: Here are some pencil sketches Khang did, which he then scanned into the computer and applied color by using digital tools such as Photoshop and Painter. The range of design possibilities for the huntsman is once again demonstrated. I hope that one of the most entertaining aspects of this project is the fact that the team and I never propose one final design for any subject. All of the designs came from reading the same story and yet they are all so different. This was the message each of the designers heard from me again and again, week after week: Be original! Not very easy to do, but special when achieved.

KHANG LE

KHANG LE

HUNTSMAN

Felix: Here I'm exploring different costume designs and time periods, trying to mix some of my own design with ancient costuming. By using graphite, I'm starting to add more details. I dropped the idea of having long drapery since he's a traveling hunter. I thought it would be inconvenient for a traveler to drag around such a costume.

Scott: Felix shows a nice range of designs that achieve that familiar yet fantastic appeal for the huntsman. His attention to detail and strong sense of graphic design help make the costume designs interesting and believable for each new direction. We have not talked much about the air gun the huntsman uses in the story, but by altering the look of this prop, Felix changes the aesthetic of the huntsman from one sketch to the next.

FELIX YOON

FELIX YOON

HUNTSMAN

Felix: After exploring various designs through thumbnails and sketches, I came up with more of a finalized look for the hunter. Here are two versions in color: a stealth ninja version and a good old hunter version.

Scott: On the opposite page are two directions suggested by Felix. I think either one would work well as the final huntsman, but since this book is all about the possibilities and processes of creating new designs we are not choosing a final. Go ahead and make your own decision for a final direction.

This spread brings us to the close of the first chapter of this book: the design development of the huntsman. At this point, I find it very enjoyable to take a quick flip back through the previous pages to remind yourself of the range of possibilities that can exist within a single story.

FELIX YOON

FELIX YOON

Khang Le 03

TRAVELS

TRAVELS

Felix: I randomly came up with thoughts and sketches of places where the hunter might have traveled. These places could be pure landscape, or could involve man-made structures. I was also experimenting with different time periods, times of day, and moods.

Scott: The design of new environments is quickly becoming one of my favorite subjects to teach and do myself when I can find the time. With this project we really let ourselves go freely to spin the story into different time periods. In addition, we wanted to consider a variety of levels of technological sophistication that the society of the time might possess. Once you make this leap into the future or the past and assume a certain level of technological ability of the people living in that place, it will feed your imagination on what the buildings, landscapes, and everything in that new environment might be like. When drawing and designing these new places, you need to be able to let your mind travel to this place and visit it in your imagination. When you get there, draw what you see.

FELIX YOON

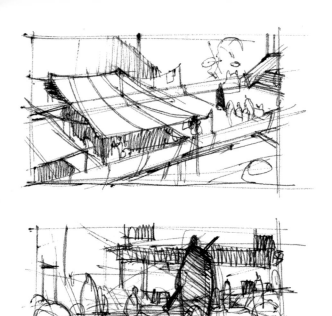

TRAVELS

Mike: When approaching the environment as a whole, I decided to create a monumental world, something of epic proportions that dwarfs the characters. I felt that this giant world could in a sense become an additional character and worked to give it a sense of history and casual grandeur. I saw the story of the huntsman almost as that of a character coming of age and discovering ones self. The locations vary in degree of cultural influence, some are more organic, some are modernist, some are crude, but I sought to include this feeling of history as though it has existed for a very long time.

Scott: Mike has a real knack for doing sophisticated graphite thumbnail sketches and value studies for his environments. On this page you can see some of the very first sketches he did for this project. I really enjoy the range of compositions and eye levels he is exploring here. You will observe in Mike's graphite work a very high level of draftsmanship that sets his thumbnails apart from most students.

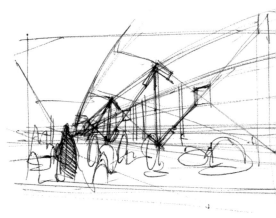

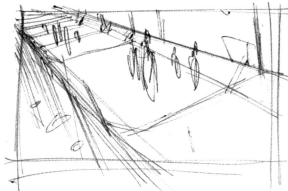

MIKE YAMADA

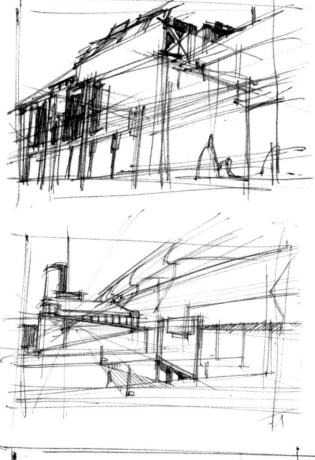

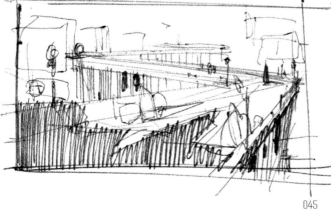

MIKE YAMADA

TRAVELS

Khang: Our favorite line in the story is a simple one, open to many interpretations: "So he traveled about and looked for work." This opens up a world of possibilities for environmental design. On this page, I imagined a giant mobile trading station. It would hover lazily across all corners of the world to buy and sell goods. The station is supported by multiple balloons. If one should deflate, the others could still maintain the giant ship. The docking process in a major town could take days for such a large vehicle.

KHANG LE

Khang: So, the huntsman traveled about. Did he find a desolate city or crumbling ancient architecture at the edge of a river? Maybe he found a snowy plain with majestic rocks, or a vibrant metropolis? I love creating worlds and imagining the life within them.

Digital painting is my current obsession for creating these worlds. It opens up a whole new way of creating images that simply wasn't possible before. One of the coolest things about this medium is the ability to use layers and bring in textures. I started this painting by putting together a collage of random images on separate layers. This created an abstract image that is the underlying structure and compo-

sition of the painting. It's fun to start with absolute chaos, and then mold it into something recognizable.

Scott: Teaching this independent study project was made very easy for me by working with such a wonderfully talented group of students. The above piece is really special. I'm glad we found that line Khang mentioned; it allowed us to include the guys' random environment sketches and renderings into a separate chapter. Hope you are enjoying this work as much as I am.

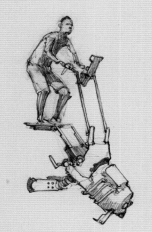
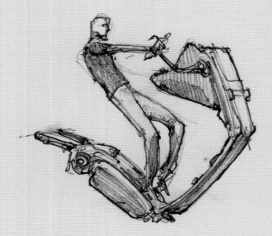
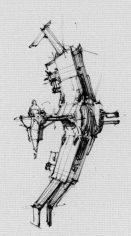
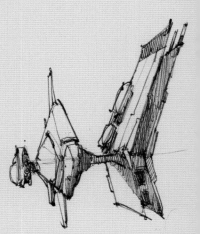

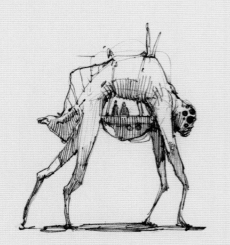

03 TRANSPORTS

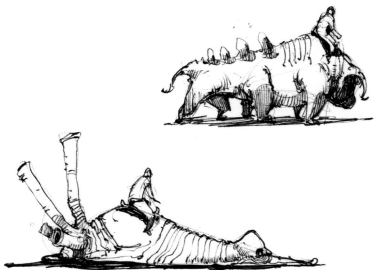
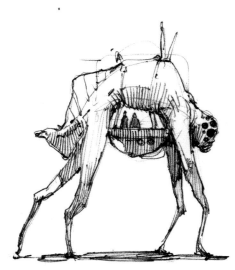

TRANSPORTS

Khang: Many of the creature transports on this page are quite ridiculous. The amount of rocking that these animals cause as they move along would probably kill the passengers. It's good to explore absurd ideas because the solutions to these problems can create new and unique ideas. It can also give the design a sense of story. For example, the spidery creature could be used for crossing a vast body of shallow water with a strong current. Using its spidery legs, it could wade across the river against the current while keeping the transport afloat. It could also lift the transport out of harm's way, away from rocks and the crashing waves, with its long, spindly legs. This is a rough ride, so perhaps the ferryman would offer to sell the passengers some motion sickness pills before the ride. It's essential to think of a story for your design while you're drawing, or else it will become lifeless.

Scott: Very well stated, Khang. Allow yourself to draw the ridiculous. You never know where it might take you or what someone else might find in your drawing.

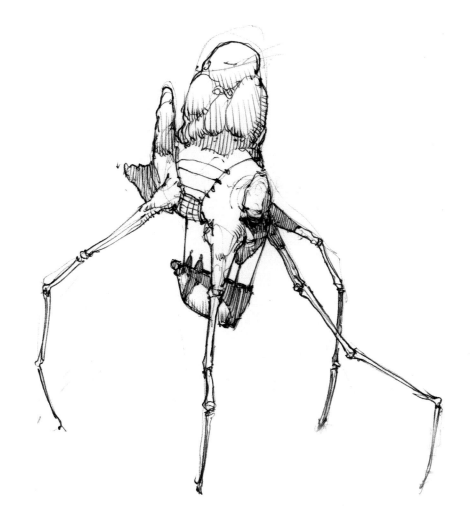

KHANG LE

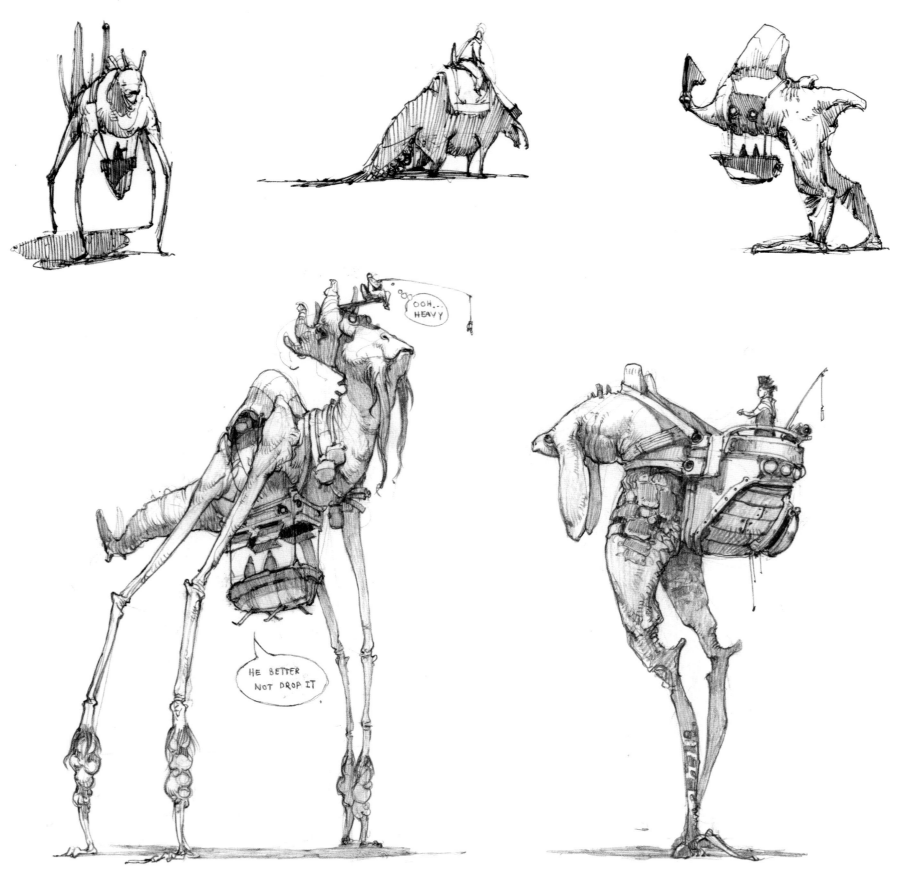

KHANG LE

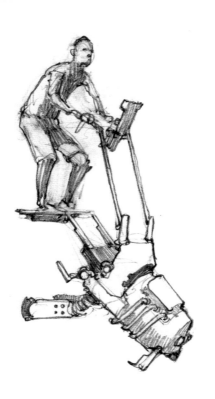
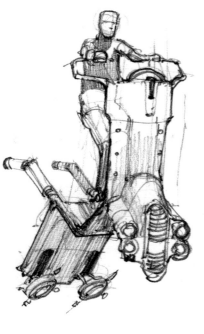

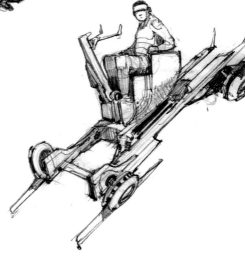

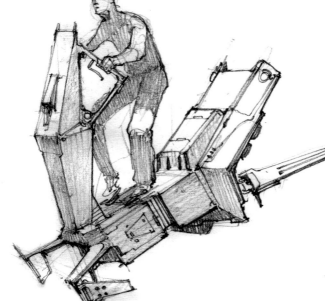

TRANSPORTS

Khang: The floating hovercraft is one of the things that audiences have come to accept in sci-fi movies. Call it anti-gravity and people will just accept it. That's the nice thing about fantastical films. You don't really have to explain how things work, just as long as they appear consistent with the fantastical rules you set forth. Mechanical design follows the same philosophy. Be consistent with any given design by giving it a set of rules. Sleek, industrial, patched up, new, symmetrical, asymmetrical, directional, nondirectional, textural, smooth —these are just some examples. These rules are the visual vocabulary that will give the design a sense of cohesion.

Scott: Khang did a nice job with these designs. The story, of course, does not talk about these exact modes of transport, but it is very easy to assume that if the story were set in the future, the huntsman would have some form of transport in that future world. I really enjoy the fact that the rider is included on most of these vehicles. It gives us, the audience, a nice sense of each vehicle's scale. His body position gets us thinking of the potential situations he might be riding into.

KHANG LE

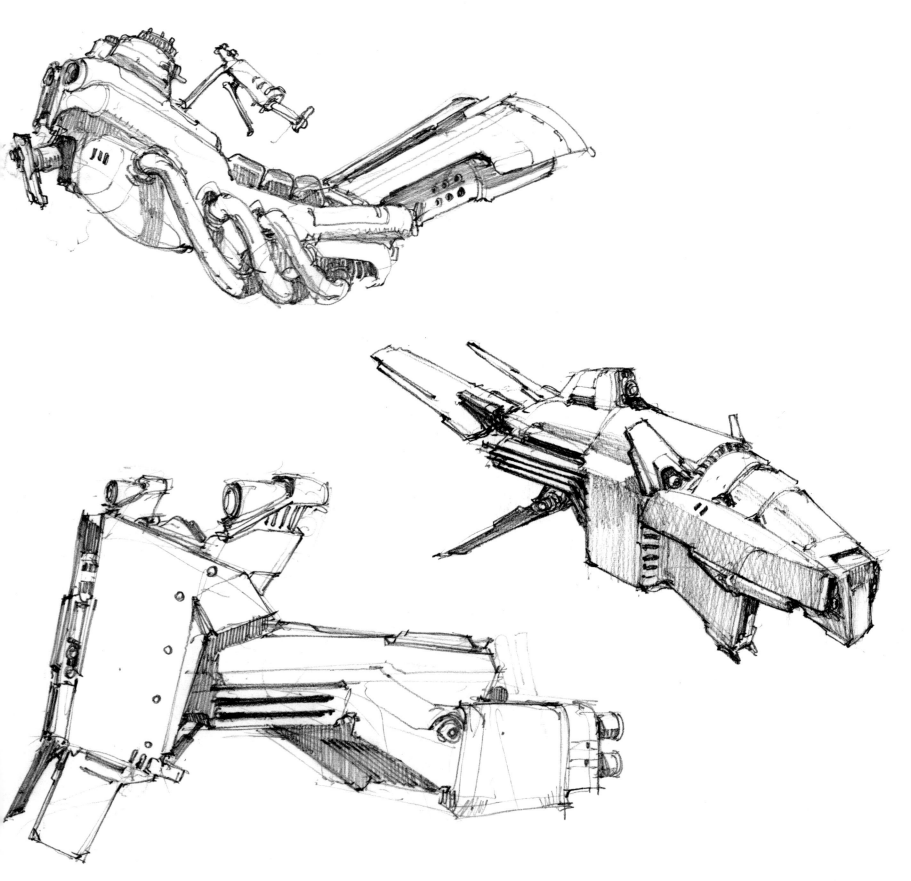

KHANG LE

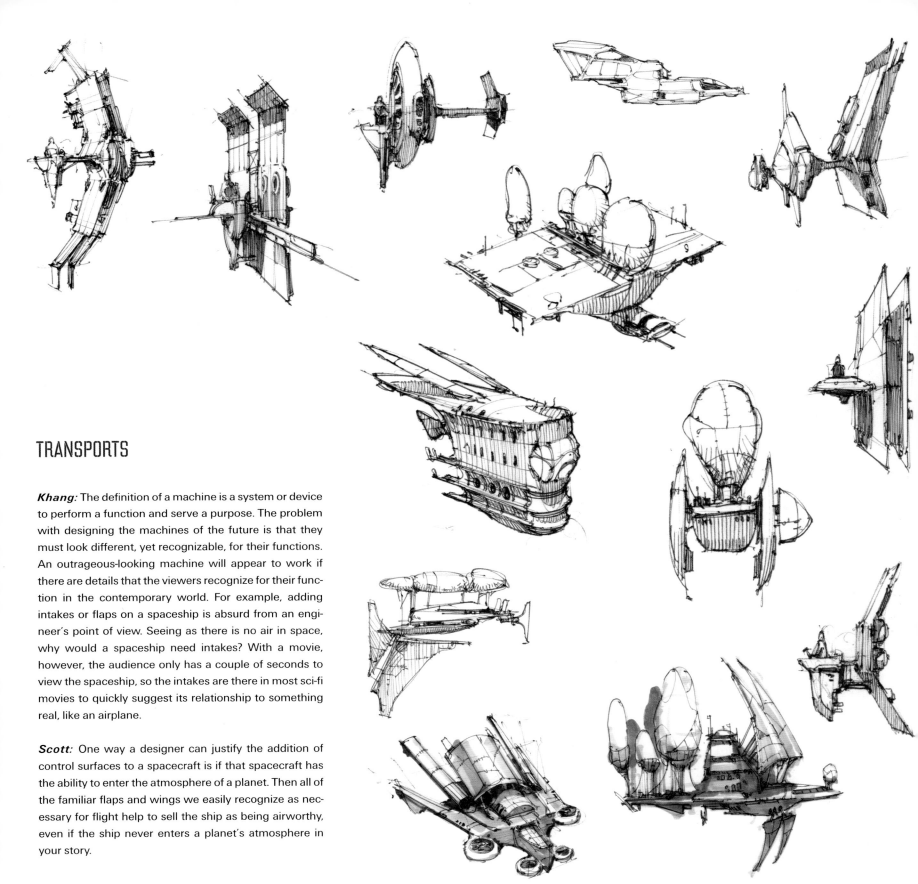

TRANSPORTS

Khang: The definition of a machine is a system or device to perform a function and serve a purpose. The problem with designing the machines of the future is that they must look different, yet recognizable, for their functions. An outrageous-looking machine will appear to work if there are details that the viewers recognize for their function in the contemporary world. For example, adding intakes or flaps on a spaceship is absurd from an engineer's point of view. Seeing as there is no air in space, why would a spaceship need intakes? With a movie, however, the audience only has a couple of seconds to view the spaceship, so the intakes are there in most sci-fi movies to quickly suggest its relationship to something real, like an airplane.

Scott: One way a designer can justify the addition of control surfaces to a spacecraft is if that spacecraft has the ability to enter the atmosphere of a planet. Then all of the familiar flaps and wings we easily recognize as necessary for flight help to sell the ship as being airworthy, even if the ship never enters a planet's atmosphere in your story.

KHANG LE

KHANG LE

04

FORESTS

FOREST

Mike: At one point I thought it might be a good idea to design monoliths for the forest, instead of designing the entire forest. The monoliths are inspired by photos of geological formations called tors and old decaying remains of columns and statues in the rain forest.

Scott: Somewhere during the development of the forest for our story we asked ourselves this question: Does the forest have to be made of trees? Could it be a forest of rocks or some other form of vegetation as yet unimagined? Sure, why not? This is a project of design process and exploration; of course a forest can be made of rocks or something all together different. On this page Mike starts out with the same process used for character development, searching for a unique silhouette. This sort of side-view, quick, thumbnail-sketching technique is fast and easy to do because you eliminate the thought needed to draw interesting compositions and perspectives. You free up more headspace to focus on design. After you have discovered a few new forms, you can integrate them into a composition, as Mike does on the opposite page.

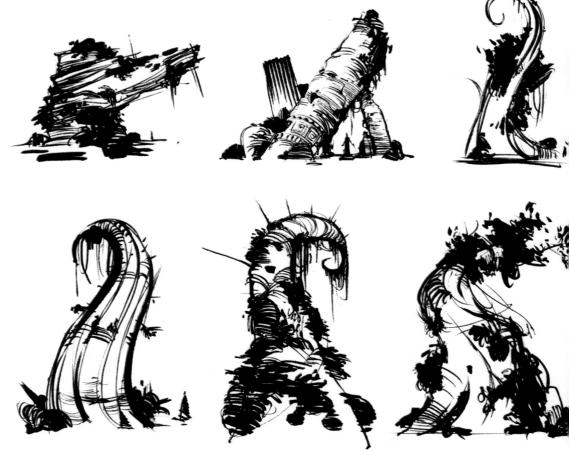

MIKE YAMADA

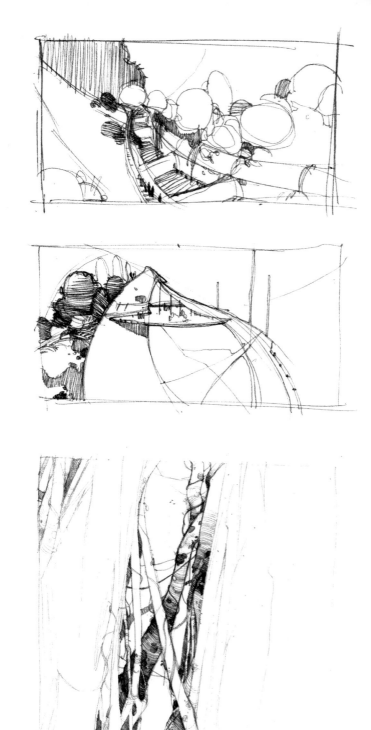

MIKE YAMADA

FOREST

Mike: The graphite tonal sketches on this page started off as extremely simple line drawings which I xeroxed and used powdered graphite to add value. Once I got to that stage I would use an eraser to remove areas that I wanted lighter and used pencil to add darks. The process itself is very organic and straightforward which allows you to concentrate on execution. The process is very therapeutic after spending hours working in Photoshop.

Scott: Mike does a clear job here of transforming his line drawings above into more realistic scenes for our story. He added value with graphite on top of enlarged copies of his sketches. Always present is the figure of the huntsman. It is human nature to scan any new image we see for signs of life, for example, other humans. Immediately we identify with the human we see in these images. Next we start to imagine what the heck might be happening to him, and, in turn, us within the image. Of course some images are more successful than others in engaging our curiosity. This is where I think the value sketch is more convincing than the line sketch. The line sketches are a kind of shorthand that we as humans can understand but can never observe in nature. They work well to convey design but not as well to convey mood or mystery; value works better for this. By leaving things out and letting our minds fill in some of the areas of the sketches on the opposite page, the scenes feel much more natural and real.

MIKE YAMADA

MIKE YAMADA

FOREST

Felix: These are some of the forests that I had in mind as I read the story. I tried to come up with a forest that we are not used to seeing. In terms of mood, I wanted a somber, quiet forest. Some of the moody ones were sketched digitally.

Scott: Applying his strong graphic design abilities to this series of sketches, Felix introduces us to a forest full of fantastic, funky life we have never seen before. Nature is the most amazing source of design inspiration. It is very helpful to draw from life and build what we call your visual library. The more you fill your visual library with interesting forms, the more you have to draw from when you sit down to imagine new things.

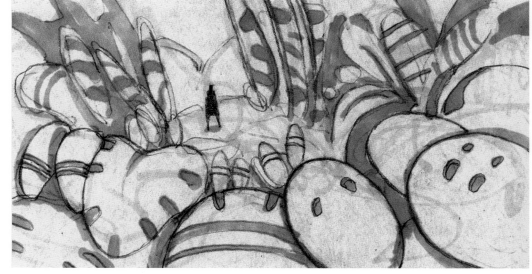

FELIX YOON

Felix: I was exploring the idea of giant orangelike fruits growing from every tree. The colored piece was a mood study of a cactus forest, which I thought should have gloomy, rainy weather.

Scott: I really like this color study Felix did. It is very different from what we see from the other designers, which once again shows the endless range of possibilities for any single item from the story. When you first look at the piece above, it seems very familiar because of the natural color palette. It is obviously very lush, wet, and we can even start to feel the cool fog on our faces. What moves us into the realm of the fantastic, even in this simple color study, is the strange shape of the things we at first think are

trees, and yet maybe they are not? Upon closer inspection they appear to be some form of giant cacti? Wait...cacti only grow in the desert, don't they? Something in this environment is not quite normal. Where are we? We are in the mind of a skilled concept designer sharing his imagination of a forest with us. Felix successfully blended the familiar, through his use of color, with the unfamiliar, through his use of form.

FOREST

Mike: The forest scenes were inspired by the work of former Disney illustrator Eyvind Earle. I tried to make nature formalized and planned much like a garden. I wanted this to provide contrast with the city, which I saw as potentially more chaotic and disorderly.

Scott: By playing contrasts against each other in the various environments, Mike makes it very clear to us where we are when we see the new natural forest environment. I think the sketches on the opposite page start to achieve a gardenlike quality. As with so much in this book, I would love to see more of these environments and see what might be the final outcome of all of this development.

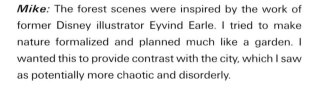

MIKE YAMADA

MIKE YAMADA

FOREST

Khang: The approach to painting a natural landscape is quite different from a cityscape. There is more emphasis on flat two-dimensional shapes instead of forms. A dense forest scene like this would be overwhelming if I tried to model the forms of every leaf and rock. Instead, I view foliage as a flat shape of contrasting value, color, and texture, overlapping into the atmospheric perspective.

The human eye sees detail on a singular focal plane. It's impossible for the eye to focus on two separate, receding planes at the same time. When painting a mass of details, pick a focal point where you'll place your details, and suggest everything around it. By simply painting a few leaves fading into a green wash of color, the whole forest is there.

KHANG LE

Khang: Nature follows very specific rules in its designs. Though it may all seem completely random and chaotic, everything in nature carries its own unique pattern. This is how we can distinguish one type of tree from another.

When designing fantastical organic life, start out by giving that thing a set of rules. The tree in the foreground has serrated discs, spikes, and roots. By consistently repeating these rules in a rhythmic pattern, the thing itself will feel natural, even musical.

Scott: Khang hits on several very important points. When designing organic forms, you need to think. Setting out a list of rules or guidelines will not only lend credibility to your designs—if you base those guidelines on nature as we know it—but it will give you the needed familiarity we have been talking about that is so important to the audience. Once you come up with a good design for a specific object such as a tree, rhyth-

mically repeat this form throughout your composition to give a more natural feel to your organic environments. Even though the organic environment seems chaotic, as Khang mentions, you can start to find very organized groupings of plant life the closer you look. It is no mistake that Khang put the fungi or spikes around each tree at approximately the same level off the ground. The repetition of form is not the only thing to look for: Observe the color patterns on plants, the height of the leaves on the stems, etc. Incorporating many of these things into your designs will give believability to your imaginary places.

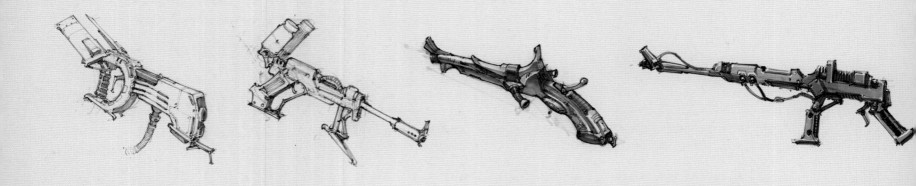

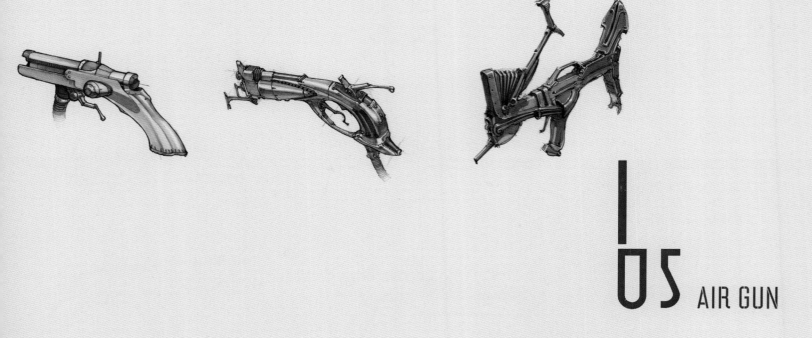

05 AIR GUN

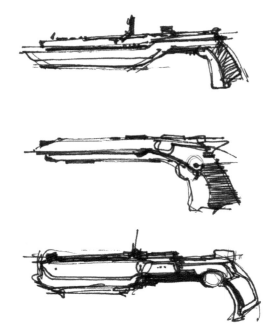

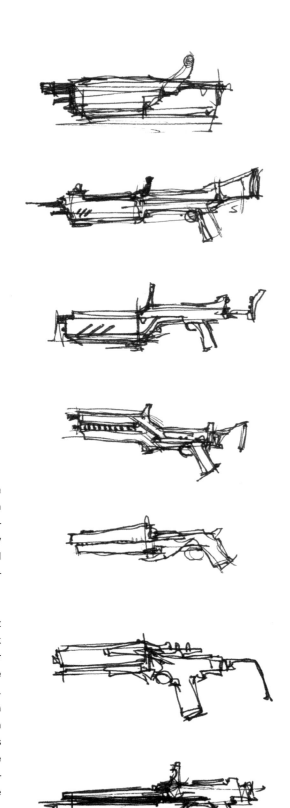

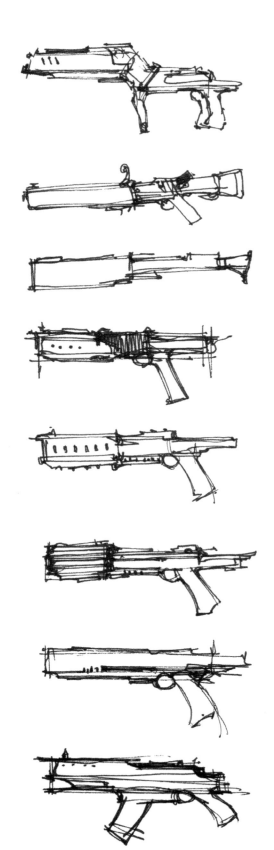

AIR GUN

Mike: I began exploration on the huntsman's air gun with several quick, rough thumbnails and decided on an approach that included both modern as well as old-fashioned components. I felt this mix of old and new would lend itself well to not being a stereotypical anime-style gun or those found in first-person, shooter-style video games.

Scott: The air gun was the most obvious and important prop from the story. Again, Mike does some quick thumbnail exploration before choosing a direction for the gun that he refines and enlarges on the opposite page. This design has a nice blend of the old and new. From the silhouette we can immediately see that it is a pistol-style gun, yet the detailing and graphic design make it more modern. Also, the attached hose hints that it is somehow a different gun than we have come to expect. The hose in this case is going to the air supply, which we would see more of later if the gun were further developed.

MIKE YAMADA

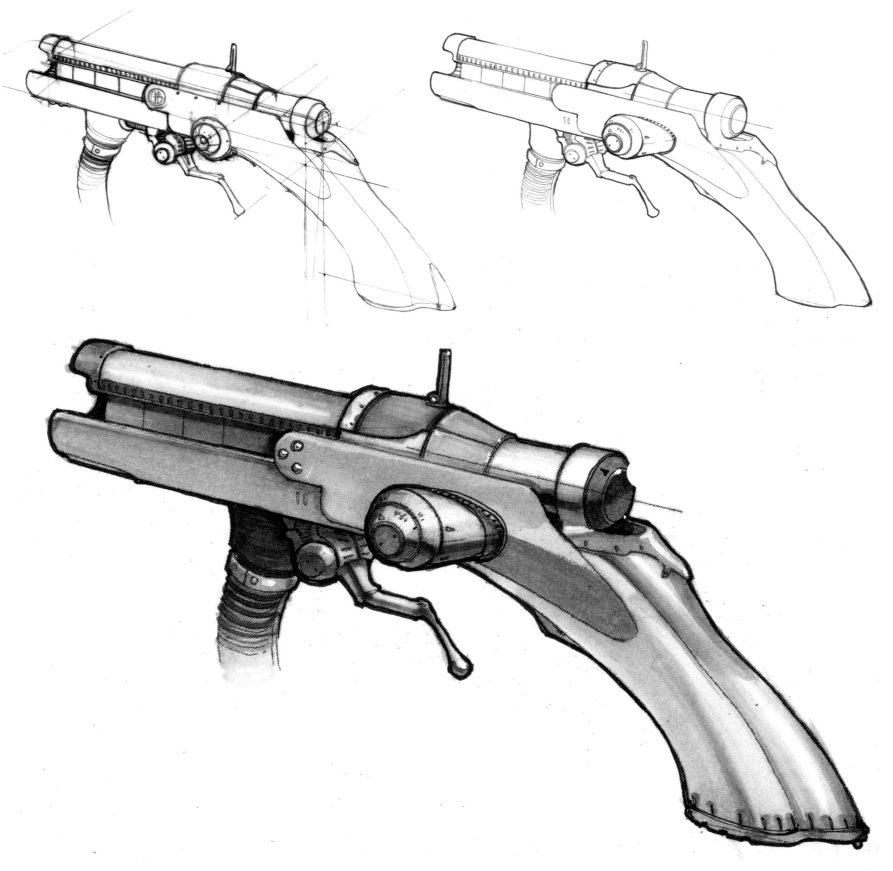

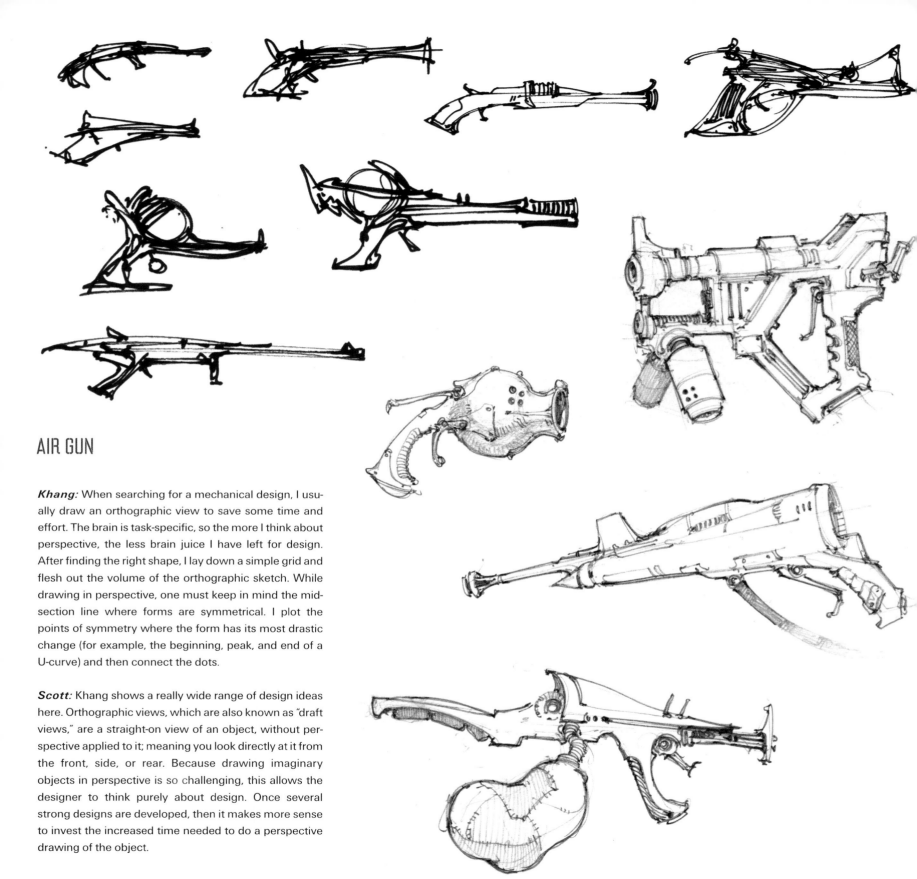

AIR GUN

Khang: When searching for a mechanical design, I usually draw an orthographic view to save some time and effort. The brain is task-specific, so the more I think about perspective, the less brain juice I have left for design. After finding the right shape, I lay down a simple grid and flesh out the volume of the orthographic sketch. While drawing in perspective, one must keep in mind the midsection line where forms are symmetrical. I plot the points of symmetry where the form has its most drastic change (for example, the beginning, peak, and end of a U-curve) and then connect the dots.

Scott: Khang shows a really wide range of design ideas here. Orthographic views, which are also known as "draft views," are a straight-on view of an object, without perspective applied to it; meaning you look directly at it from the front, side, or rear. Because drawing imaginary objects in perspective is so challenging, this allows the designer to think purely about design. Once several strong designs are developed, then it makes more sense to invest the increased time needed to do a perspective drawing of the object.

KHANG LE

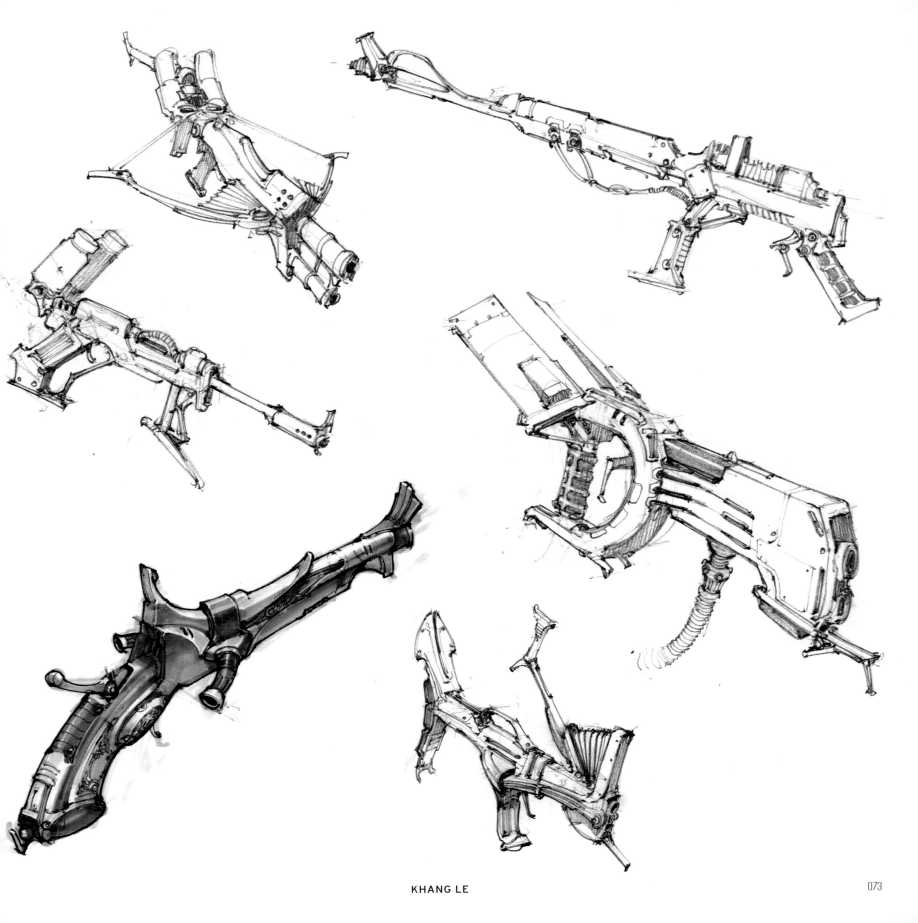

KHANG LE

073

AIR GUN

Khang: I wanted to have some fun with the air gun. Instead of having the air supply come from a run-of-the-mill air tank, I thought it would be interesting to see it come from an organic source. Imagine that there are little creatures that live in the forest who have a defense mechanism whereby they create compressed air and fluff themselves up to appear larger to predators. The huntsman catches a big batch of these creatures, yanks their tails to force them to inflate, sticks them onto the air chamber of his gun, and fires away. After the shot, these creatures are too exhausted for another immediate use. They need a couple hours of rest before the huntsman can use them again. After about ten or so usages, they become tasty jerky for the journey.

Scott: This is a really fun page. The drawings define a comedic sequence of use for our poor, little air-supply creatures. What is most enjoyable about all of the designs in this book is seeing the countless directions any of the visuals in a story can take when a talented team of concept designers is set to task.

KHANG LE

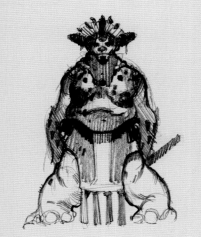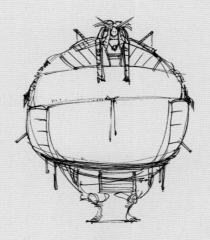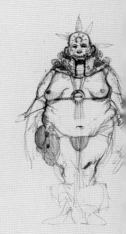

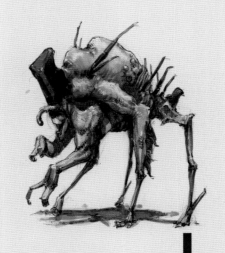

06 GIANTS

GIANTS

Mike: Just like the huntsman character, I began designing the giants by sketching silhouettes. But unlike the huntsman, I was not limited by the realities of the human figure. Giants can look like anything. So I started with abstract shapes, much more abstract than the ones used for the huntsman. Actually I was inspired by T-shirt designs, and worked to make this block-formed creature. I wanted the giants to be disturbing. They needed to be human enough to be relatable, but different enough to be mysterious.

Scott: Mike starts out with the fantastic here in his silhouette sketches. As a designer, I love to look at this type of sketch because so much of what is on the inside of the silhouette is left to my imagination. This type of sketch is usually only used by the individual designer to help generate those all-important first ideas, and is not shown to others unless they are also designers and a part of the visual development team.

MIKE YAMADA

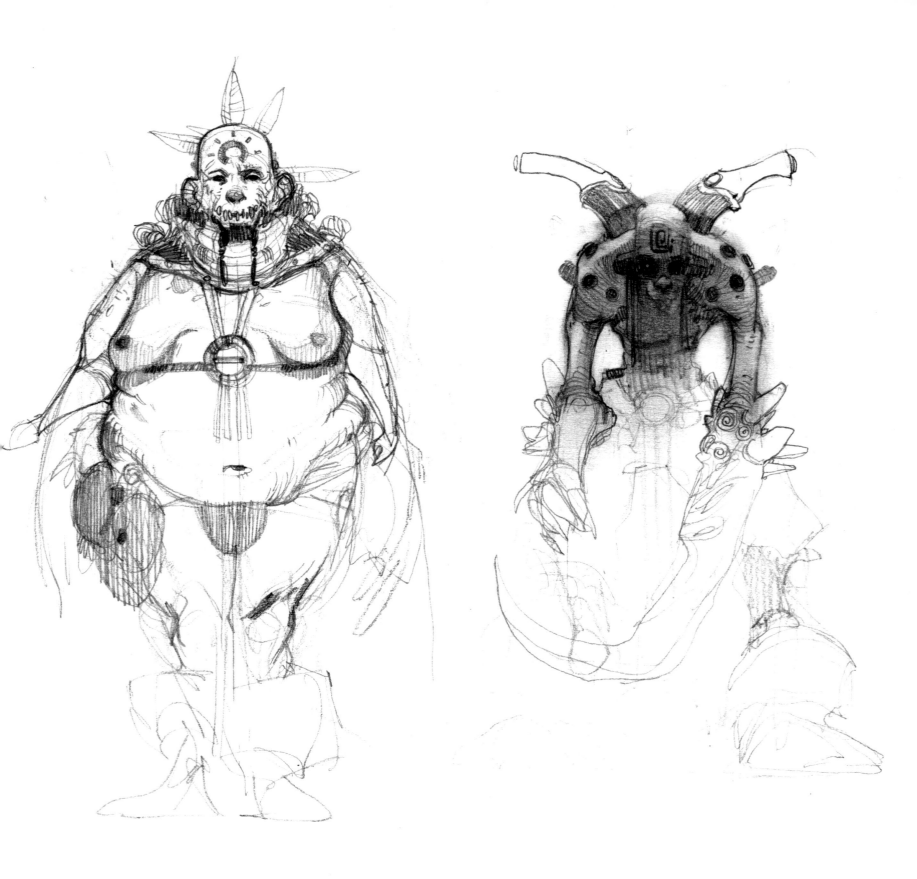

GIANTS

Mike: I attempted to give the giants a brutal, primitive quality. I wanted them to be savage, wild characters, but not be archetypally evil. I was working with making their outfits organic and also medieval in a way—a primitive sort of styling.

Scott: Mike makes a solid start here toward developing a new, tribal aesthetic for his giants. I'm not sure what is growing on top of that giant's head at the top of the opposite page, but I like it because I have not seen it before. The growth also offers something fresh and immediately identifiable about the character design of one of the giants.

MIKE YAMADA

MIKE YAMADA

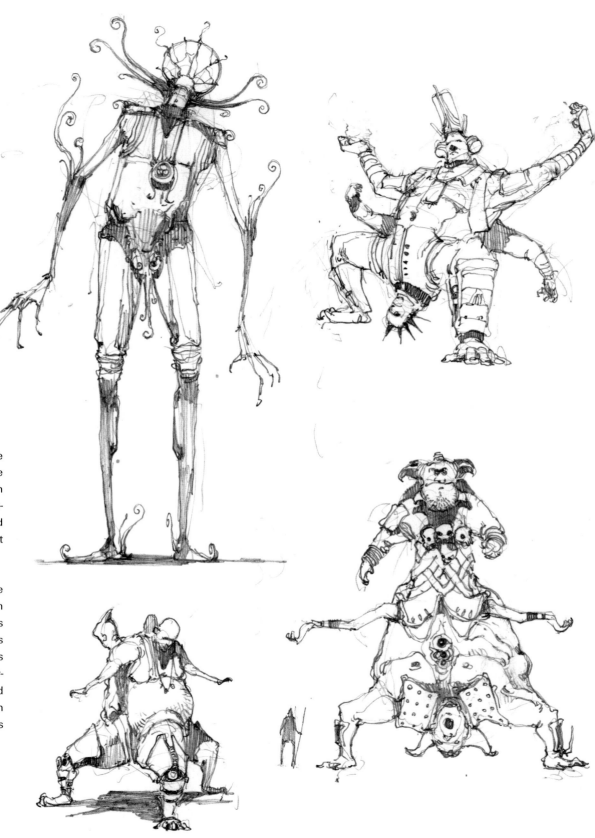

GIANTS

Khang: For these sketches, I'm toying around with the idea of the giants sharing the same body. It would be interesting to see how this affects their movement with two or three different mind-sets. I also gave them contrasting design elements within the same body. It would be humorous to see them constantly bickering about simple daily choices.

Scott: Khang does a great job of playing with the scale of the giants and the abstract forms they might take. I'm not sure how some of them would get around, but at this early stage we don't worry about that too much. This is the time to focus on putting down as many original ideas as possible. Even when a design might seem too far-fetched or not that well-defined, it may provide a good starting point for another designer to take off and run with it. For that reason, no sketch is edited out at this point of the process.

KHANG LE

KHANG LE

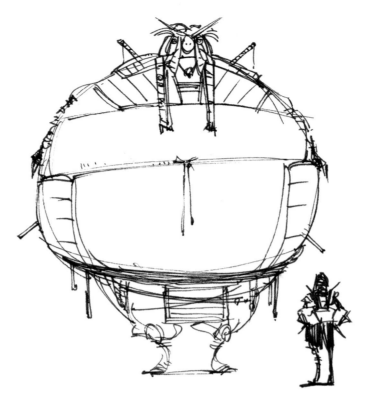

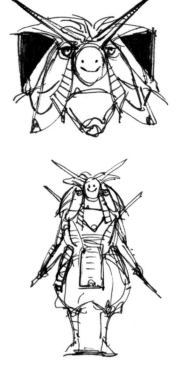

GIANTS

Felix: Basically, I wanted the giants to be humanoid creatures that are huge and bizarre-looking, but have a tribal feel as well. They do travel in a pack, after all. My favorite is the fat giant with a weird face that is unrecognizable. Color was added in Photoshop.

Scott: Felix mixes it up here not only by exploring the scale of the giants, but how thin or fat they may be as well. I find the early stage of a development project to be the most exciting and fun to do. We are following our story, which provides us with our list of characters, vehicles, props, and environments to design. Beyond that there is only the imagination of the designer who interprets the story and shares his ideas of what the contents of the story might look like.

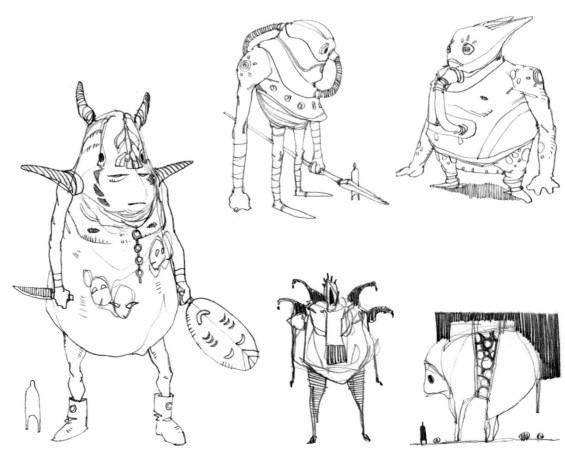

FELIX YOON

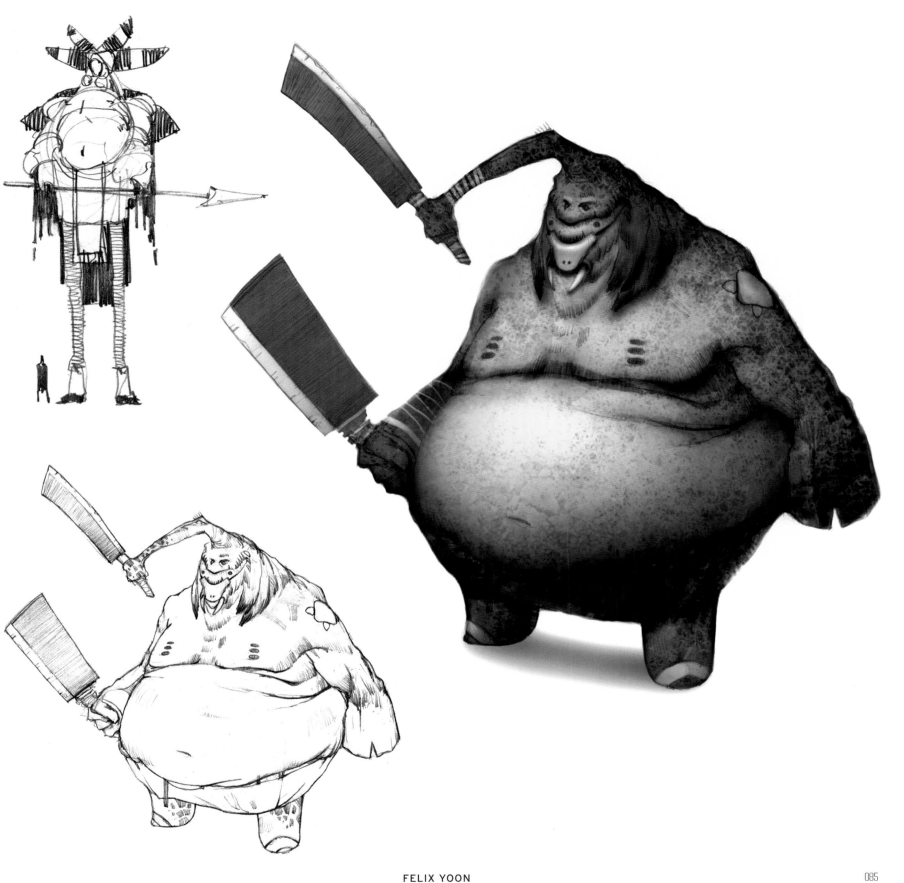

FELIX YOON

GIANTS

Khang: One of the approaches for character design is to do the headshots first, then design the body around the aesthetic of the head. Once I can see what sort of personality the creature has, I can better judge what sort of costumes he should wear. On the right side are some colors choices for the same sketch. Color combinations change the look of the creature: pink flesh, leathery skin, stripes, spots. The varieties are endless.

Scott: Most of the time, after a viewer quickly takes in the general pose and silhouette of a character, the next place he or she will look is the face. Knowing this, Khang spends some design time here on the potential heads we might see on the giants in our story. Color is very key in conveying the personality or mood of a character. How do you feel the character's personality changes on the opposite page as the colors change?

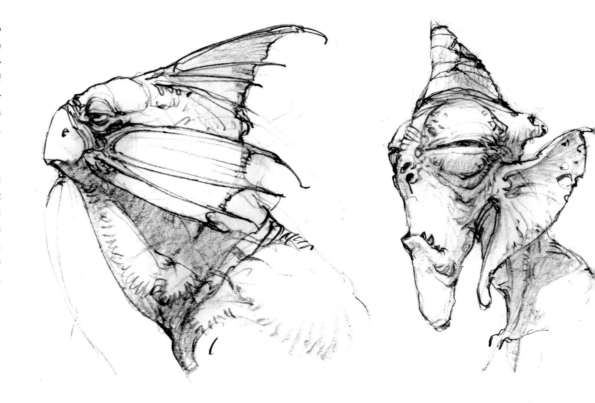

KHANG LE

KHANG LE

GIANTS

Khang: My favorite is on the far right. I like the way it was rendered and its simple silhouette. The arm texture was done by painting with a clone brush from a scanned oilpainting. I enjoy working with traditional sources and digital tools. It's a very liberating process that allows room for spontaneity.

Scott: The giant on the opposite page was a late addition to this chapter, and I think it has an appropriate scale in relation to the huntsman, and enough human qualities so that I, as an audience member, can easily relate to it.

KHANG LE

07 CASTLE

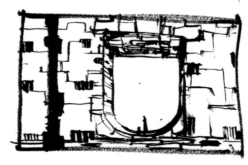

CASTLE

Mike: As with the characters, I tried to apply the same abstract approach to designing the environments. Here I wanted to create a combination of grandiose and intimate spaces. I also wanted to contrast it with the "formalism" that I put into the forest scenes, and apply some degree of organic nature to the castle. The castle should feel somewhat familiar, but still regal.

Scott: This page is a great example of early sketches a designer would do usually just for his own viewing to flesh out a new direction. Since our book is about that process, we're happy to share them with you. Mike does an interesting job of using the arches as an architectural design element. We all "read" them as being regal, yet they are upside down here, which hints at a castle or world where things are different from what we have come to expect here on Earth.

MIKE YAMADA

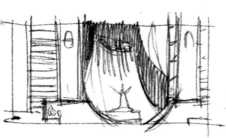

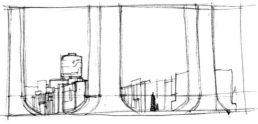
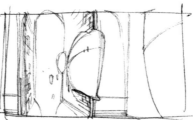

MIKE YAMADA

CASTLE

Khang: As a child, I loved building with Legos and making origami. I think those fond childhood memories have a lot to do with why I'm so obsessed with visual construction. On the left are some orthographic thumbnails for the castle. I often approach each design with a few visual vocabularies such as round, geometric, asymmetrical, etc. Then I find the musical rhythm of the drawing and harmonize the individual details.

Scott: Even though Khang is designing a castle, he can still employ the draft-view sketching technique you have seen throughout the project to free up his mind and arrive at an interesting design before he jumps into perspective on the opposite page.

KHANG LE

KHANG LE

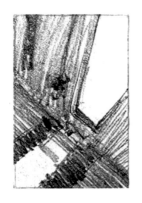

CASTLE

Felix: This is the scene when the huntsman enters the princess' bedroom. I sketched out scenes with different compositions and lighting and ended up liking the dramatic bird's-eye view. This lets us observe the scene without being in it, and makes the moment between the huntsman and the sleeping princess more intimate. I wanted the scene to have an elegant Art Nouveau quality, which is why I stuck with curving shapes.

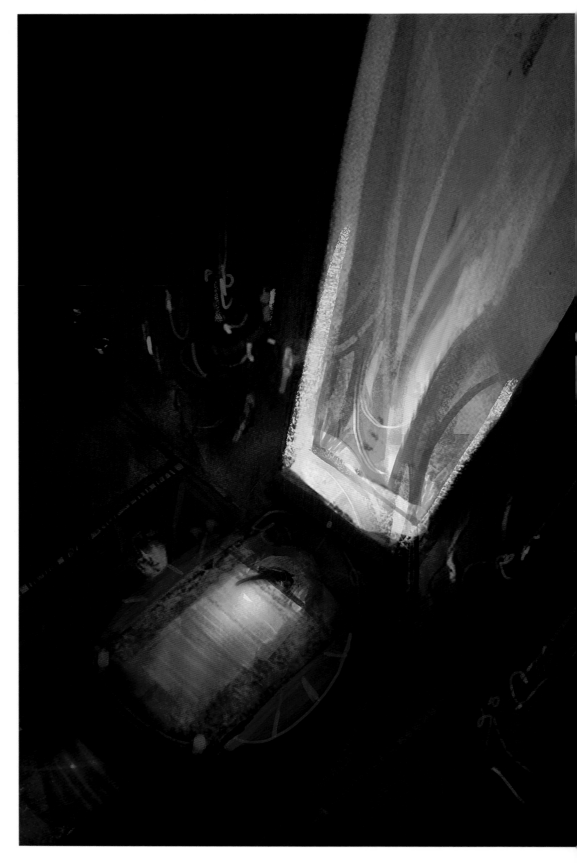

FELIX YOON

Felix: Here is the entrance to the princess' bedroom. I wanted the scene to have a dreamy and somewhat futuristic feel. I used dramatic lighting to convey the right mood.

Scott: I love this color sketch for the mood it conveys about the type of place our huntsman is about to enter. It looks very large, and Felix and I discussed the addition of a figure somewhere to make that more obvious. But even without one, I feel the amount of atmosphere he has added conveys the immense scale of the space. From a technique point of view, it is fun to do these types of one-point-perspective, symmetrical compositions by copying and flipping your original sketch in the computer before you start to paint color on it. You can see some of the sequential steps Felix saved along the way to completing this piece.

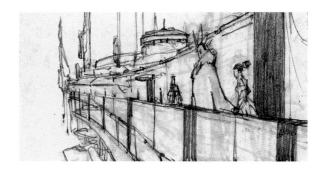

CASTLE

Felix: Here, the setting is the castle stairway where the huntsman picks up the sword. I wanted to give a solemn, Gothic feel while keeping the fairy-tale-like dreamy quality. The heaviness of the staircase evokes the power of the king, the marble communicates his wealth. If you can imagine the huntsman entering this hall, perhaps he would feel a bit intimidated by the grandeur, which serves to contrast with the huntsman's relative anxiety or courage. All angles aim toward the focal point of the room, the sword. As the huntsman ascends the stairs, he becomes more and more vulnerable to discovery. After doing some initial sketches and value studies, I finalized the color piece, which was done in Photoshop.

Scott: This is one of my favorite pieces that Felix did for the project. If you look closely at the color piece, you will see that he pulled off a very realistic look to the space using a strong value range and a minimal amount of detailing.

FELIX YOON

FELIX YOON

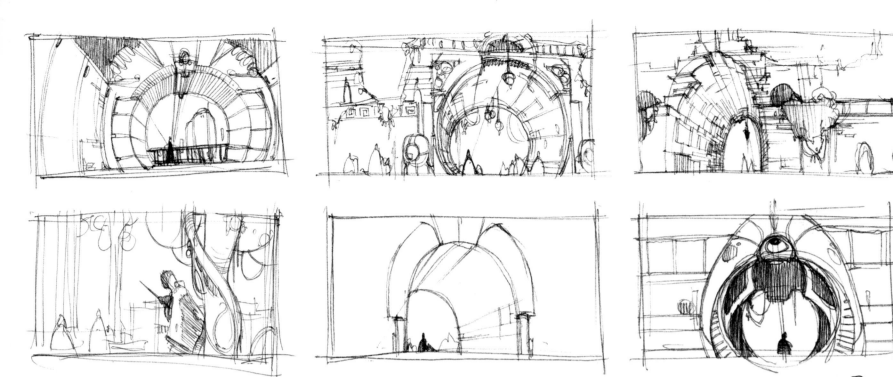

CASTLE

Mike: I was trying to explore this idea about a secretive side entrance into the castle; something almost like a sewer tunnel or an aqueduct. It needed to be very simple, abstract, and moderately organic, yet not. It becomes a nice transitional space between a more formal environment (forest) and a more chaotic one (castle). Basically I drew on an organic approach to classical architecture with a bit of the French comic artist Moebius thrown into the mix.

Scott: In the story, this could be the entrance the giants squeeze through into the castle courtyard where the huntsman finishes them off. Mike again shows a high level of detailing in his thumbnail sketches. I like how he dropped the top half of the huntsman's body into shadow in the value sketch to the right, effectively making him feel like the earlier silhouette sketches that were so successful.

MIKE YAMADA

CASTLE

Felix: In this room of the castle, the captain meets the king. I tried to visualize the scene while keeping it loose. The dramatic perspective view shows the magnitude of the interior, making it more imposing.

FELIX YOON

Felix: This late afternoon shot is how I visualized the exterior of the castle, with a lake surrounding it. The birds in the background give some movement to the image, and are light and ephemeral while the castle is solid and staid. The birds are free to stay or go and do as they please; the princess who resides here is not.

Scott: Felix took a more historical approach to the design of the castle. Even so, I feel the design is strong, familiar, and at the same time new and intriguing. When designing a period piece, it can be very difficult because everyone already knows what the thing should look like. If you stray too far from familiarity, the piece will not feel correct to your audience. Felix walks the line expertly here.

CASTLE

Khang: For the castle's interior painting, I went with a geometric-and-Art Deco aesthetic. I kept the colors to a minimum to emphasize the rigid forms of the structures. The castle painting on the right is an homage to a picturesque shot of James Gurney's *Dinotopia*. I wanted to create a harmonious blend of nature and human architecture. I designed the architecture to resemble sea corals growing on pier bridge supports.

Scott: These are some of my favorite pieces that Khang did for the project. More than anything, I think what he accomplished was a great sense of scale in the environments. The painting on the right, with the round, beehive castle forms, feels fresh from a design perspective. The bright colors suggest a festive atmosphere.

KHANG LE

GUARD DOGS

GUARD DOG

Felix: I explored various ideas and directions for the guard dog. I had a messed-up, brutal creature in mind. First of all, it needed to be mean enough to have discouraged three giants. And its appearance would give us an idea of the even greater potential dangers lying ahead for the huntsman.

Scott: There is quite a diverse range of techniques shown on this page, any of which could be explored further to realize the full potential of the medium. At the top, the use of texture and the color really helps to convey a very disturbed and brutal guard dog. I thought the black silhouette studies were interesting, and since this book is about the process of creating the visuals, and not just about showing finished final designs, they work well as starting points for further exploration either by Felix or one of the other guys.

FELIX YOON

Khang: The dog was a small character in the story. I wanted to make this character very much like a family pet. It would be funny to see that three giants were afraid of and deterred by a cute, little pup. For the sketch to the left, I thought it would be interesting to see a creature with large front legs and flimsy hind legs. I'm curious to see how this creature will move when animated. How will it sit, jump, pee? With fluffy hair covering its mouth, it'll be adorable to see it growl as its muzzle fur vibrates. The creature at the bottom of the page is like a clumsy pig. Being raised by a rich, royal family has made this creature obese. I thought it would be funny to see this "dog" get shot by the air gun and go belly up.

Scott: Khang took a decidedly humorous approach, and I agree with him that it would be very fun to see any of these dogs animated and scaring off the three giants.

KHANG LE

09 PRINCESS

PRINCESS

Mike: To create options for the design of the princess, I once again relied upon silhouette-based thumbnails along with some of the more traditional variety. I was attempting to accomplish this difficult balance between graceful/feminine and awkward/immobile. These were mostly quick sketches focusing on ideas and possible approaches to making her unique.

Scott: Mike shows us a nice variety of shapes and sizes with the sketches on both of these pages. When I look at the black silhouette sketches on the opposite page, I like to try to imagine the reverse view of the figure as well. Meaning, am I viewing the figure from the front or from behind?

MIKE YAMADA

MIKE YAMADA

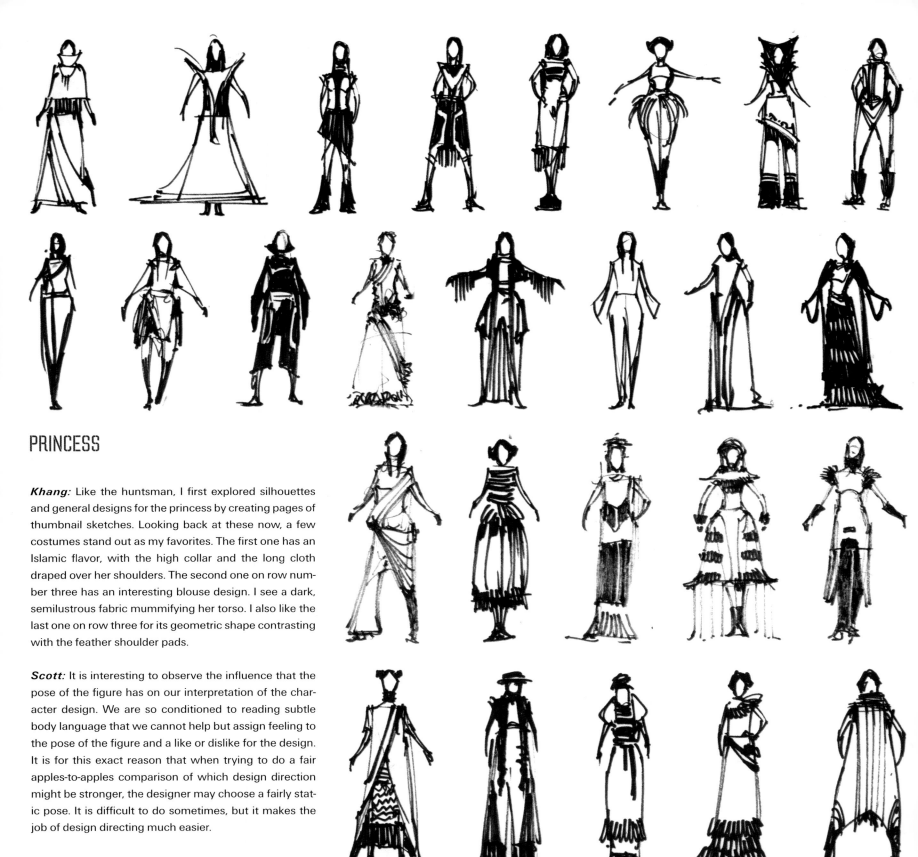

PRINCESS

Khang: Like the huntsman, I first explored silhouettes and general designs for the princess by creating pages of thumbnail sketches. Looking back at these now, a few costumes stand out as my favorites. The first one has an Islamic flavor, with the high collar and the long cloth draped over her shoulders. The second one on row number three has an interesting blouse design. I see a dark, semilustrous fabric mummifying her torso. I also like the last one on row three for its geometric shape contrasting with the feather shoulder pads.

Scott: It is interesting to observe the influence that the pose of the figure has on our interpretation of the character design. We are so conditioned to reading subtle body language that we cannot help but assign feeling to the pose of the figure and a like or dislike for the design. It is for this exact reason that when trying to do a fair apples-to-apples comparison of which design direction might be stronger, the designer may choose a fairly static pose. It is difficult to do sometimes, but it makes the job of design directing much easier.

KHANG LE

KHANG LE

PRINCESS

Mike: I was very inspired by sketches done by Iain McCaig and Dermot Power in the *Art of Star Wars: Episode II: Attack of the Clones* and tried to give the princess a similar feel. I played with contrasting large areas of flowing fabric with bound areas. I wanted her to be noble and proud, but also to give slight hints of contradiction. As we know, she eventually renounces her royal lifestyle to go live alone in the forest.

Scott: Mike successfully mixes the bound and flowing fabrics in the sketches above. What is so intriguing to me in now observing this entire block of artwork in one book is how the same drawing process can work so well for so many different subjects. Once students can see that conceptual design is about a process and an approach to an idea, then I think they are unafraid to explore the design of any new subject. At the core of designing anything visual, you can always start with the proportion of the object's silhouette, and then move inward by adding the graphics. Most young designers don't realize that graphic design is a huge part of entertainment design. Last on the list of development is the surfacing.

MIKE YAMADA

MIKE YAMADA

PRINCESS

Felix: While designing the princess, I kept in mind that I wanted the people who dwell in the castle to have an opposite style from the hunter. Since the hunter that I drew had an old, ancient style to him, I wanted the princess to be very clean, sleek, and elegant. I tried to incorporate bold yet simple graphic designs into her costumes.

Scott: Looking at Felix's sketches of the princess' dress, it is again evident how powerful the practice of strong graphic design can be for the entertainment designer. Choosing a style theme and repeating that theme throughout the costume is a very traditional approach to creating something universally perceived as being attractive.

FELIX YOON

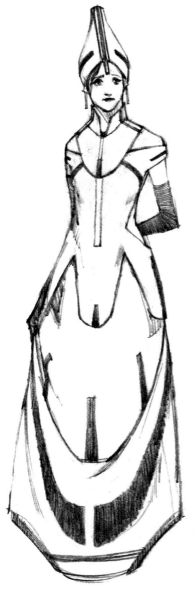

FELIX YOON

PRINCESS

Felix: This page explores more options for the princess, with more detail and emphasis on the facial expression. Some sketches show her as a peasant. The color drawings were painted in Photoshop.

Scott: I enjoy how Felix is starting to impart the personality of the character now though the use of color. The designs have moved out of the thumbnail phase and into more refined proposals for the direction the princess' character design might take.

FELIX YOON

FELIX YOON

PRINCESS

Khang: For this princess painting, I found a texture to use as an underlayer for the pattern of her fabric. The dark deep-red was just an accidental choice while I was collaging random images in Photoshop. It's great when these happy accidents occur. The possibilities of visual design are so unlimited; sometimes it's better to leave things to chance. It saves a lot of headaches that way.

Scott: More headdresses and multiple design directions for the princess shown here by Khang. Again, since our project and this book are about the process of creating the visual elements of our story, I find it very interesting to see all the potential directions for the princess design. Maybe we will be lucky enough to see the final designs of each chapter in another version of this book or in a film someday.

KHANG LE

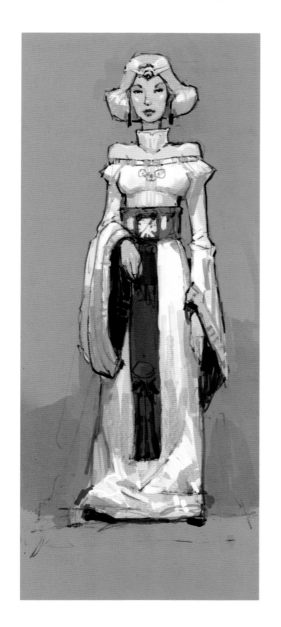

KHANG LE

10 KING

KING

Khang: I love drawing headpieces. You can definitely go wild with the design since he's a king, so the more elaborate, the better. Though some of these designs would be too cumbersome to wear if they were made for a movie, I try not to limit myself when doing design. It's better to worry about the actual physical properties later. The four headpieces have their own sense of character. The first is noble, the second is mysterious, while the third and fourth are feminine and spiritual.

Scott: There is not much to add here. Khang does a thorough exploration of what the king could be like in our story. I really like the upper-left sketch on the opposite page. I can imagine the silhouette of that king would be very imposing indeed.

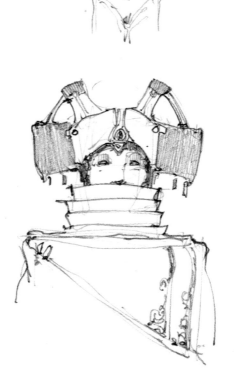

KHANG LE

KHANG LE

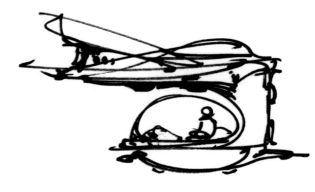

KING

Khang: Ever since I read the *Dune* book about the evil baron, I thought it was very cool that he had a personal vehicle to move him about in his palace. I wanted the king in this story to have the same type of mobility. Maybe his legs are too weak for walking much in his large castle, or maybe he's just lazy. Whatever the reason, I drew some thumbnails to explore the variety of shapes of this vehicle. My favorite of these is the sketch on the right side of the page, the middle sketch. It has a majestic awning-shape along with a glass bubble that befits a king.

Scott: These sketches are really fun. I like the variety of shapes and sizes. Some don't look proper for a king, such as the large toilet he is riding around in on the opposite page at the top. Khang's choice of which one to develop was a good one as we will see in the coming pages.

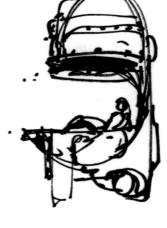

KHANG LE

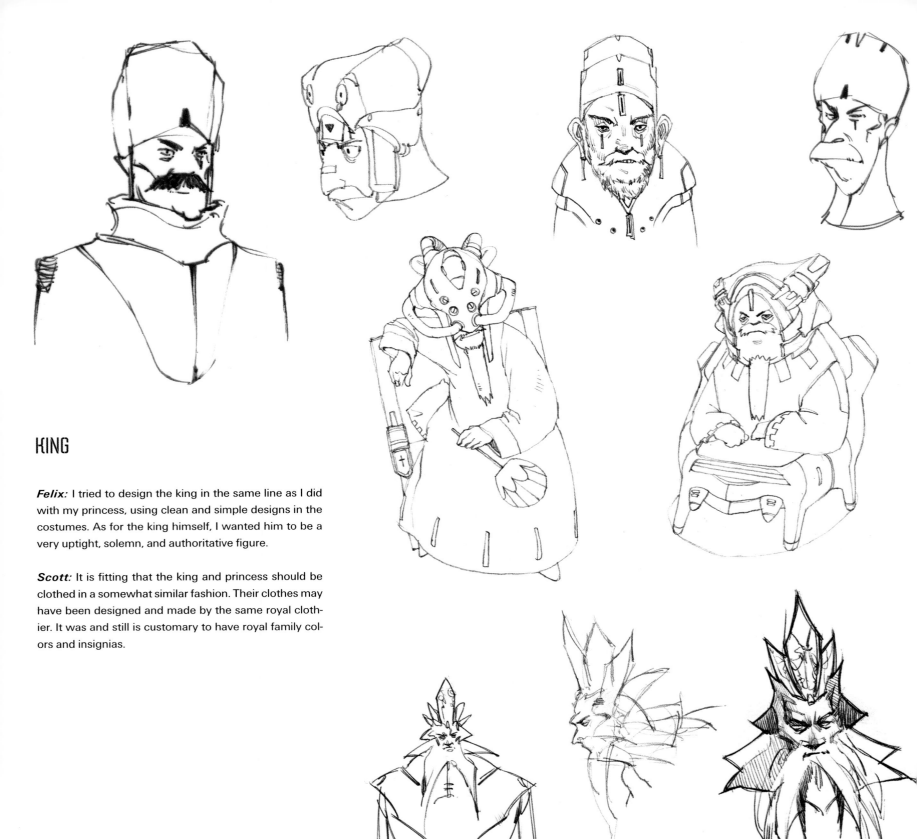

KING

Felix: I tried to design the king in the same line as I did with my princess, using clean and simple designs in the costumes. As for the king himself, I wanted him to be a very uptight, solemn, and authoritative figure.

Scott: It is fitting that the king and princess should be clothed in a somewhat similar fashion. Their clothes may have been designed and made by the same royal clothier. It was and still is customary to have royal family colors and insignias.

FELIX YOON

FELIX YOON

131

KING

Felix: These are colored versions. I wanted to convey the right expression and mood while keeping the image loose. Loosely placed brush marks are making things look believable at a glance. The use of lighting is also helpful in creating a realistic realm.

Scott: Felix has a nice style on both of these color renderings. Through the use of dramatic lighting on this page, he is able to influence our perception of the king's personality. He is not someone I would like to have dinner with. Also of note in Felix's rendering work is the way he tricks your eye into believing that the design is much more finished than it really is. Look closely at the subtle material indication of some of the surfaces, and you can see that a carefully placed reflective highlight here and there can do a lot to convince us of a highly polished surface or a material change.

FELIX YOON

FELIX YOON

KING

Khang: Here is the hover throne, also known as the "love bubble." For these two designs, I kept the surfaces smooth and curvy to reflect the majestic nature of this vehicle. A few ornamental touches, like the flag, statues, and draperies, add to the aesthetic.

My process for rendering these images starts out with a gray marker, like Copic #2, to get the general perspective and shape. I will then go to a #4 to reinforce the basic forms. For dark shapes, I use #6. Finally I use a small, black-ink pen for the details. The thin, white highlights were drawn with a white milky pen sold in most art stores; they help to tighten the sharp details.

Scott: I have always liked the very sculptural qualities of the king's costume on the opposite page, and was pleased that Khang chose this one to render in color. It is quite common to see the most ridiculously impractical clothing worn by royalty for specific ceremonial events; I think the tilted waistline plane of this costume falls perfectly into this category.

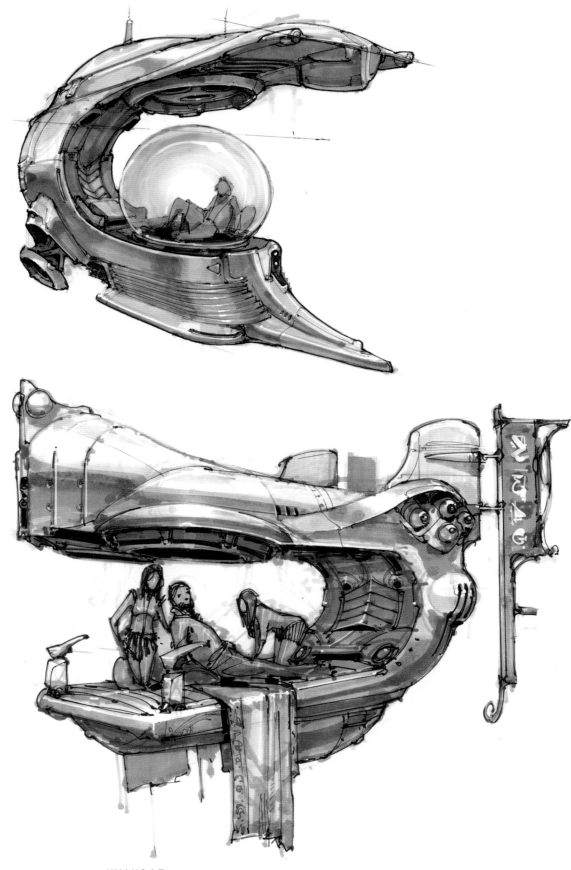

KHANG LE

KHANG LE

11 CAPTAIN

CAPTAIN

Khang: The evil captain was very fun to do. You can get more far out when the character is supposed to be dark and menacing. I started out with some pure-black silhouettes. They help to define the overall shape of the character. My favorite sketch from this page is number three on the first row. It just seems very original, and its repeating dark bubbles remind me of the beady eyes of a spider. I also like the fifth sketch on the first row because it reminds me very much of the baron from *Dune*. He's a shady, fat midget who's up to no good.

Scott: Portraying evil is a much easier job than portraying good. Aggressive, mean-spirited characters are easier to draw and design because we can easily overexaggerate their personalities; they become stronger icons of evil full of danger, mystery, and excitement. It is much more difficult to convey good in an enticing way that can equally capture an audience's interest.

KHANG LE

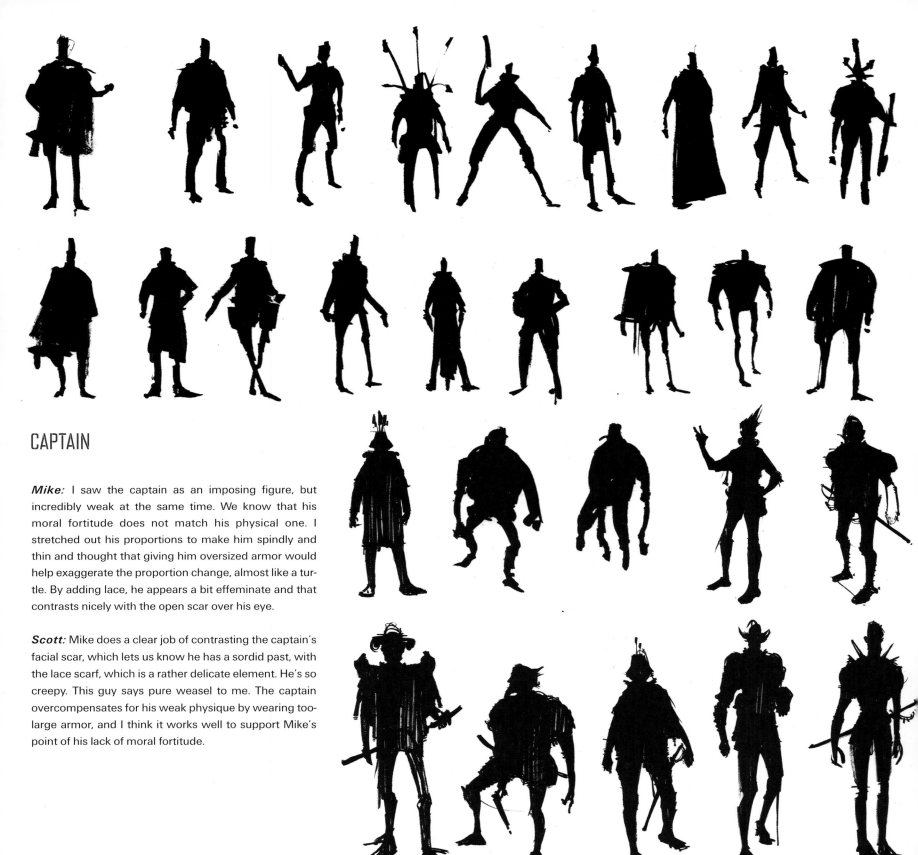

CAPTAIN

Mike: I saw the captain as an imposing figure, but incredibly weak at the same time. We know that his moral fortitude does not match his physical one. I stretched out his proportions to make him spindly and thin and thought that giving him oversized armor would help exaggerate the proportion change, almost like a turtle. By adding lace, he appears a bit effeminate and that contrasts nicely with the open scar over his eye.

Scott: Mike does a clear job of contrasting the captain's facial scar, which lets us know he has a sordid past, with the lace scarf, which is a rather delicate element. He's so creepy. This guy says pure weasel to me. The captain overcompensates for his weak physique by wearing too-large armor, and I think it works well to support Mike's point of his lack of moral fortitude.

MIKE YAMADA

MIKE YAMADA

CAPTAIN

Felix: I kept in mind that the captain would be a wicked, greedy character, so I tried to express that as much as possible in most of the sketches. I ended up liking him in a robe with a religious look to it. This image of good contrasts well with his evil motives. In the color piece, I wanted to capture a vicious facial expression that would represent his true character.

Scott: Felix does a great job of playing up the angularity of the captain's facial features. Generally speaking, people view round shapes as friendly and angular shapes as mean or aggressive. Knowing this before you start a character design can make an easier job of communicating the personality of a character through the proportion and form of his features. For example, look at the captain holding the apple to the right. Note the round, smiling face. Now compare this to the smiling captain above. Which one looks more wicked and evil?

FELIX YOON

FELIX YOON

143

CAPTAIN

Khang: In the above sketch I have a very classical, European ornamental costume contrasting with his future-punk hairdo and face mask. There is something about him that is devious but sympathetic at the same time. In the sketch to the right, I reinforced the spider-eyes idea and made the costume color like that of a black widow. I imagined his suit to be rubbery with a brown stain throughout the crevices.

Scott: I really like the design of the captain on this page. The spider-eyes chest plate is a fresh approach for this character's costume. The faces on the opposite page better convey a cold, evil character through the use of cooler colors for his skin tone. Again, back to a round-versus-angular form of language; you can see that the greenish guy on the opposite page has an immediately more recognizable evil edge to his personality.

KHANG LE

KHANG LE

COOKHUT

COOK HUT

Mike: These two pages represent two different approaches to coming up with a design for the cook hut. This page shows a silhouette-based approach where I paid most attention to the groupings of masses as well as the gesture. On the accompanying page, I used a normal line-based sketching style and focused mostly on unique details and proportion.

Scott: Again, we can see Mike exploring various silhouette designs with the thumbnail technique for his take on the cook hut. Looking at the sketches on this page, see how your own imagination fills in the rest of the design for the interior of the silhouetted cook-hut forms. Looking at the opposite page, observe how the lines and graphic shapes now seen on the interior of the sketch become the areas where our eye looks first. Both of these techniques work well and allow a designer to explore different areas of the design based on how our brains will differently interpret each type of sketch.

MIKE YAMADA

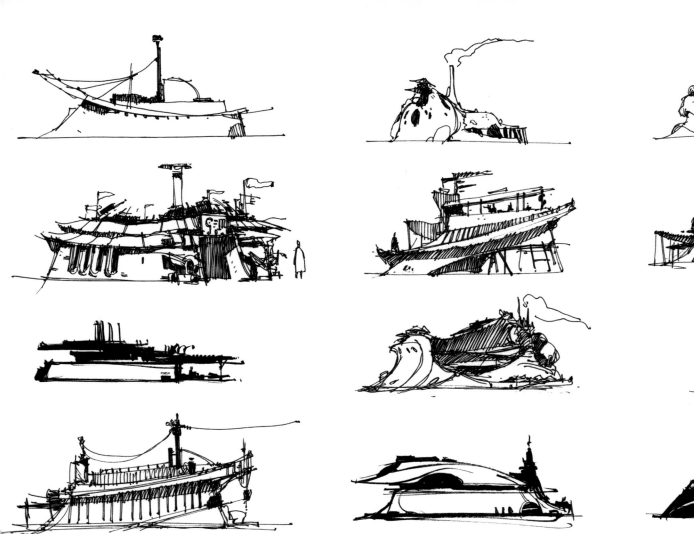
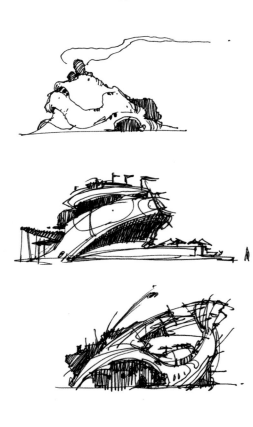

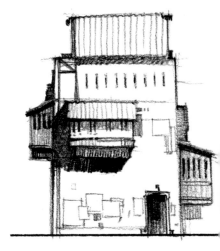

COOK HUT

Mike: I tried to explore many directions for the architecture, contrasting organic shapes with artificial ones, and trying various states of disrepair. I narrowed the idea from a fairly large structure to something more like a taco stand or a small burger joint.

Scott: Refining the sketches from the previous page, Mike brings us a little closer to the cook hut by adding more design details and a little value to the sketches. I like the idea of the cook hut being rather small and in stark contrast to the prior digs of the princess. Also, it is nice to see such a range of shapes, both organic and more geometric, for design solutions to the same piece of architecture in our story. It makes it hard to pick a final direction; many of these could be worked up into a solid final design for the story.

MIKE YAMADA

MIKE YAMADA

COOK HUT

Mike: I looked at the cook hut as something fairly large, maybe the size of a small house. I wanted to include some subtle or small indication of her previous royalty as well as appearing aged and worn. I experimented with various small details as symbols of her former position in life including banners (possibly emblazoned with the crest of the royal family) or architectural forms reminiscent of classical architecture.

Scott: Mike has chosen a few designs to take further by adding some color to his previous sketches. The color sketch at the right is one direction for the cook hut. When depicting a specific design for a story, it is common at this part of the object's development, in this case the cook hut, to do very simple backgrounds in a color sketch so as to put the focus on the design versus the depiction of the scene that might be happening during the story. Mike has done a bit of both here by adding figures to the sketch. We see the huntsman exchanging a few words with the princess. The figures hint at story point very well and show the hut's scale.

MIKE YAMADA

COOK HUT

Felix: I explored a lot of designs and shapes for the cook hut. I wanted the exterior to have a cozy, inviting feeling. The interior painting was done to illustrate the mood for the cook hut. I wanted to convey the deserted feeling; the princess yearns for company. She is alone but she has not given up hope, as she faces the entrance and the light. How long will it be until the answers are revealed to her?

Scott: A wide range of shapes are shared with us through the sketches on this page. The interior sketch on the opposite page really sets a mood for the space with the strong green palette. The image is so strong, I really want to see more sketches of the scenes to follow in this cook hut's interior.

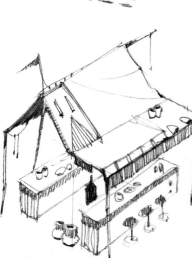

FELIX YOON

FELIX YOON

COOK HUT

Khang: I wanted the cook hut to have a handmade, organic feel. I enjoy seeing architecture that is not planned but built and modified through the ages as necessity dictates: metal sheets to protect from the rain, chimneys that puncture through rooftops, irregular shapes that create a sense of evolution and history. That's my biggest problem with Los Angeles architecture—everything seems new and sterile. Buildings are constantly being demolished instead of being modified. They resemble simple Lego blocks and are devoid of personality.

Scott: Like Felix, Khang shows a good range of designs here, and pulls off a strong interior piece on the opposite page. With extra attention put into the detailing, such as the trophy heads on the far wall, we can almost smell this place. It is now ready for some figures to act out their roles.

KHANG LE

COOK HUT

Khang: I would love to see this building animated. All the piping rumbling, the loose metal plates flapping about as the cook tries to cool a simple loaf of bread. The pencil is still my favorite tool for organic drawing. There's just no better substitute for the variety of marks this simple tool can make. It's practically the only physical tool I use now, besides my digital Wacom tablet. I really haven't found a faster way of getting visual ideas out of my head.

Scott: Great point made by Khang. Drawing with an old fashioned pencil is still very, very hard to beat for the sheer simplicity and speed with which you can record your ideas and share them with others. All good design first starts with an idea and then is conveyed to your audience with strong drawing and then rendering skills. Over and over I have observed with my students that strong drawing skills go hand in hand with strong design skills. Good drawings support better-looking designs.

KHANG LE

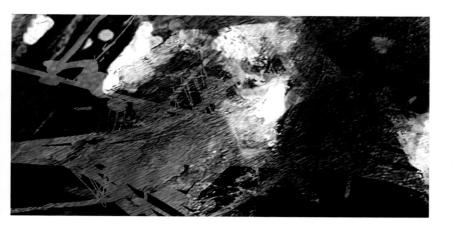

Khang: Here you can see how I progress from abstraction to final illustration. The first image was a random digital collage of various images on separate layers. I learned this technique from my illustration class at Art Center under David Luce. He asked us to splat some ink randomly on a page, and create a recognizable image out of the abstract pattern. It was a very fun exercise, and I apply the same method in Photoshop. The process is actually even more limitless in the digital format because of the infinite availability of images on the Internet. For example, randomly place a photo of a piece of modern architecture over a Vincent van Gogh painting. Crop a small area, and you might see a very strange image that will spark your imagination. I really love this process since it takes me beyond the limits of what feels comfortable. These strange shapes and textures will act on my memory and knowledge of things I have experienced, and open my mind to a new place that can take me by surprise.

Scott: This process works great for the creation of interesting environments. With the use of so many digital visual tools, this process is even faster and more fluid than it has been before. Give it a try if you are into painting environments, and I think you will find it can really enhance your range of compositions and design.

closing remarks

We hope you have enjoyed this look at the entertainment design process as demonstrated by Khang, Mike, and Felix. It has been my great pleasure to work with them, and I'm eager to watch their professional development within the entertainment design industry. I hope that one of the most entertaining aspects of this project is the fact that the team and I never settle on one final design for any subject. All of the designs came from reading the same story, yet they are all so different. This was the message the designers heard from me again and again, week after week: Be original! Not very easy to do, but special when achieved. We hope to bring you many more books like this one. If you are interested in learning more about the design and drawing techniques presented in this book from professional entertainment designers, please visit www.thegnomonworkshop.com to view our broad selection of educational DVDs.

Best of luck with your own work.

Scott Robertson

---

other titles by design studio press:

Exodyssey:
visual development of an epic adventure
paperback ISBN:
978-1-933492-39-1

Framed Ink:
drawing and composition for visual storytellers
paperback ISBN:
978-1-933492-95-7

The Daily Zoo:
keeping the doctor at bay with a drawing a day
paperback ISBN:
978-1-933492-34-6
The Daily Zoo Year Two:
paperback ISBN:
978-1-933492-44-5

MY Daily Zoo:
a drawing activity book for all ages
paperback ISBN:
978-1-933492-63-6

Daphne 01:
the art of daphne yap
paperback ISBN:
1-9334-9209-0
hardcover ISBN:
1-9334-9208-2

Structura:
the art of sparth
paperback ISBN:
978-1-933492-25-4

Alien Race:
visual development of an intergalactic adventure
paperback ISBN:
978-1-933492-23-0

Luminair: techniques of digital painting from life
hardcover ISBN:
978-1-933492-24-7

The Art of Darkwatch
paperback ISBN:
1-9334-9201-5
hardcover ISBN:
1-9334-9200-7

Lift Off:
air vehicle sketches & renderings from the drawthrough collection
paperback ISBN: 1-9334-9215-5
hardcover ISBN: 1-9334-9216-3

Start Your Engines:
surface vehicle sketches & renderings from the drawthrough collection
paperback ISBN: 1-9334-9213-9
hardcover ISBN: 1-9334-9214-7

Drive:
vehicle sketches and renderings
paperback ISBN:
978-1-933492-87-2

Concept Design 2:
paperback ISBN:
1-9334-9202-3
hardcover ISBN:
1-9334-9203-1

designstudio PRESS

To order additional copies of this book and to view other books we offer, please visit:
www.designstudiopress.com

For volume purchases and resale inquiries please e-mail:
info@designstudiopress.com

Or you can write to:
**Design Studio Press
8577 Higuera Street
Culver City, CA 90232**

tel 310.836.3116
fax 310.836.1136

Instructional DVDs by **design studio press** and **the gnomon workshop**:
Authored by **Scott Robertson**

To order these DVDs and to view other DVDs we offer, please visit:
www.thegnomonworkshop.com